PEACE WITH CHILD CARE

"CREATIVE CHILD CARE in my lovely Green Hills home..." In 1975, Jean Byler McCracken placed this brief classified ad to run for one day in Nashville's afternoon paper. She received forty-three calls from very interested parents, proving what she had suspected from experience: A lot of parents were scrambling to find better child care. At first, her home-based day care served four children, but the relentless demand for her services called for something more. Within months, she relocated and developed one of the leading child care programs in her community, where she served for nearly three decades.

IF YOU ARE LIKE hundreds of parents who talked with Jean McCracken in her child care center office—or the thousands more she had to turn away on the phone due to a lack of available space—then you know your search for appropriate child care is one of the most difficult things you've ever faced.

You know there's more to your day care decision than location, cost, class size, and a license to operate. The usual checklist is an important starting point, but what are the deeper quality indicators? What are you not thinking of? What's most important? How will this experience affect your child? To achieve peace of mind about the decisions involved, you need a seasoned expert to share inside information—you need secrets to finding day care you can trust.

IMAGINE YOURSELF RELAXING for an hour-long Q&A over coffee with a leading child care provider. What would you ask her? How valuable would that counsel be for your family as you begin your search for child care?

In *Peace with Child Care*, veteran child care provider and author Jean McCracken goes much deeper about all you're facing than she ever could with parents on the phone or even during hour-long armchair discussions in her office.

She has poured twenty-seven years of experience onto the pages of *Peace with Child Care* and provides the answers you need to begin feeling reassured rather than overwhelmed.

In *Peace with Child Care*, Jean McCracken helps you

- take an objective look at whether to use day care at all;
- discern what distinguishes higher-quality child care programs from the ones parents ought to be unsettled about;
- influence the best care you find to become even better for your child;
- understand why she says, "What your child needs most in day care is *free*";
- And more.

JEAN BYLER MCCRACKEN is the former managing owner of Creative Learning Center in Nashville, Tennessee, where she worked with parents and caregivers to invest in the lives of young children. Although she never expanded her business beyond a single large child care center, her program's excellent reputation did attract unsolicited invitations and requests for proposals to provide child care services for leading organizations, including GM's first Saturn™ plant and Vanderbilt Stallworth Rehabilitation Hospital in Nashville. She and her husband, Alan, have two grown sons.

"ALL parents seeking child care for their little one should read this book first!"
—*Nashville Parent Magazine*

PEACE WITH CHILD CARE

*Secrets to Finding Day Care You Can Trust
From a Veteran Child Care Provider*

Jean Byler McCracken

www.faithwellpress.com

Faithwell Press
PO Box 158943
Nashville TN 37215

Copyright © 2007 Jean Byler McCracken.

All rights reserved. No portion of this book may be reproduced, stored in a retrieval system or transmitted in any form - electronic, mechanical, photocopy, recording or by any other means, whether now known or later developed - without the prior written permission of the publisher, except for brief quotations in printed reviews.

Scripture quotations are from The Holy Bible, English Standard Version, copyright © 2001 by Crossway Bibles, a division of Good News Publishers. Used by permission. All rights reserved.

Faithwell Press, its logos and the FP colophon are trademarks of Faithwell Press, Inc.

Cover design by Gore Studio, Inc. | www.GoreStudio.com.

Cover photo © Jamie Grill/Corbis.

LCCN: 2007922027

ISBN: 978-0-9790349-1-6

*To my husband, Alan,
and our sons, Michael and David
– men of mercy, all.*

ACKNOWLEDGMENTS

I am indebted to my late parents, Rev. and Mrs. James Emerson (Shirley) Byler, for their commitment to appropriate child care services for young children. They supported three churches' decisions to offer these services to their communities. My first glimpse of the joy in this work came through one of those programs.

I'm also especially thankful for my brother, Judson Byler, and his wife, Rebecca—gifted educators who led our program for several years in the 1980s. Creative Learning Center flourished under their leadership. After they moved on, we continued much of what they developed there and will always be grateful to them.

In addition, so many parents supported my efforts with patience and kindness while I learned how to manage and administer a child care program. Thanking all of them would require its own book. Somehow they recognized that when I missed the mark and got it wrong, I was trying to get it right.

I deeply wish that I could name every caregiver—each one whose heart was inclined toward little children—who did her work on the children's behalf as unto God, when no one else ever saw it. I want you to know that I saw it, even when I wasn't present in your classroom, because the result was reflected in the expressions of confidence and contentment on your children's faces every day. Those kind and caring people who worked closely with us at CLC providing administrative and managerial support on our behalf, and those who cooked for the children and who provided other support services were a vital part of our efforts there. May God bless each of you for what you have done for children.

Special thanks to the book's editor, Carrie Andrews, for her wonderful work and for providing an editorial process that was much easier and more fun than I ever dreamed possible.

Finally, I want to thank my family, whose encouragement and prayers supported and sustained me in my work at Creative Learning Center. Thank you, beloved Alan, for all you did to help me establish a child development center in 1976 and, later, for taking time away from a successful career to manage that center for several years when I was unable to do so. For always loving and believing in me, I am forever grateful.

Thank you, Michael and David, for the countless times you came to our rescue at the center to help us do what we could not have done alone. I am also deeply grateful to you both for your involvement and support in this book project. Thanks, Michael, for your insight and honesty when I needed to "tone it down a little" in certain passages. And thanks, David, for the many hours you spent helping ensure that what I had written was actually communicating. Thanks to all three of you for persisting—each in your own way—until I finally gave in and wrote this book.

CONTENTS

🌿🌿 INTRODUCTION 17

PART ONE

The Need for Child Care and How Mothers Really Feel About It 23

1. THE MOTHER'S HEART 25
   - What Happens while You're Making Plans 26
   - Social Acceptability and Personal Anguish 27
   - Why Is This so Hard? 27
     - The Fundamental Problem 28
   - One Mother's Great Expectations 29
     - A Wonderful Memory 29
     - A Painful Memory 30
   - Family Life as It Used to Be 31
     - Two Servants 32
     - No Perfect Families 33

2. WHY WE NEED CHILDCARE 35
   - America's Workforce 36
   - Very Personal Reasons 37
   - Other Financial Reasons 38
     - Taxes 38
     - Housing Costs 38
     - Health Care Costs 39
     - Life versus Lifestyle—My Personal Mistake 39

3. WHY YOU NEED CHILDCARE 41
   - Evaluating Dreams 42
   - Real Life in the Grown-up World 43
   - A Decision Only You Can Make 44
   - Unresolved Feelings and Unrealistic Dreams 44
   - The Decision to Stay at Home 46
     - Counting the Cost 48
   - The Decision to Use Child Care Services 49
     - True Guilt versus False Guilt 49
     - Grief 50
     - If It's Best for Your Family, It's Best for Your Child 51

PART TWO

What the Young Child Really Needs and How to Find It 53

4. WHO IS THIS DEVELOPING CHILD (AND WHAT DOES HE REALLY NEED)? 55
- First Things First—Your Child's Developmental Needs 56
- Have I Found the Right Center If He Likes It? 57
- The Nature of This Decision 57
- The Nature of the Young Child 58
- How Can I Know What to Look For? 59
- Who the Child Is Not 59
- An Adult-in-the-Making 60
- He Needs to Learn How to Learn 61
- Appropriate Developmental Support 61
  - He Needs to Develop Language 62
  - He Needs Social and Emotional Development 63
  - He Needs Pre-Academic Skills 65
  - He Needs to Develop Motor Skills 66
  - He Needs Creative Expression 67
  - He Needs to Be Protected 68
  - He Needs Discipline 70
  - He Needs Good Values 78

5. STARTING YOUR SEARCH 81
- Referral Resources 82
  - Regulatory Departments and Referral Agencies 82
  - Family, Friends, and Associates 82
  - Churches and Other Religious Organizations 83
  - Grade School Teachers 84
  - The Internet 84
  - The Director of the Program You Can't Get Into 85
  - The Yellow Pages™ 85
- Gathering Basic Information 86
  - Making the Call 86
  - Is Space Available? What About a Waiting List? 86
  - Ask One More Question 88
- Quality Clues over the Phone 88
  - Be Prepared—Getting through May Take Time 88
  - Listen for Quality Clues 89
  - Background Sounds 90
- Schedule a Tour 90
  - Prepare to Focus on What You See 91
  - The Midmorning Tour 91
  - The Lunchtime Tour 92
  - The Midafternoon Tour 94

PART THREE

Inside the Business of Child Care 97

6. CENTER POLICIES 99
    What a Policy Statement Reveals 100
    Child Care Centers and Theme Parks 101
    Child Care Centers and Hospitals 102
    It's Not Child's Play 103
    What a Strong Policy Statement May Look Like 103
        The Nature of the Organization 104
        Hours of Operation 104
        Paperwork Parents Provide 104
        Emergency Procedures 106
        Arrival/Departure Procedures 107
        Upholding Your Caregiver's Rules 108
        Impaired Drivers 109
        Tuition and Fees 109
        Insurance 110
        Trial Enrollment 110
        Withdrawal 111
        Center Policy Changes 111
        Notices to Parents 112
        Parent/Staff Communications 112
        Absences 113
        Illness 113
        Medications 114
        Meals, Snacks, and Foods from Home 115
        Toys from Home 115
        Outdoor Play 116
        Change of Clothing 117
        Parent/Staff Relations 117
        Discipline 118
        Staff Turnover 119
        Policies for Parents of Infants 121
        Policies for Parents of Toddlers 122

7. WHO'S WATCHING OUT FOR YOU?
    LICENSING, RATINGS, AND ACCREDITATION 123
    The Necessity of Regulation 125
    Licensing 127
    Going Beyond the Basics—Ratings and Accreditation 128
        Star Ratings 128
        Accreditation 130

Other Regulatory Oversight Agencies 130
    The Fire Department 131
    The Health Department 131
    The Codes Administration 132
So Who's Watching out for You? 133

PART FOUR

The Tour 135

INTRODUCTION TO THE TOUR 137

8. THE NEIGHBORHOOD, BUILDING, AND GROUNDS 141
    The Neighborhood 142
        Safety 142
        Proximity to Emergency Services 143
        Noise Pollution and Other Hazards 143
    The Building and Grounds 144
        First Impressions 144
        Is the Interior Space Inviting? 145
        Can You See into All Classrooms? 145
        Are Buildings and Grounds a Community Asset? 146
    The Playground 146
        Basic Playground Structure 146
        Why the Playground Is So Important 147
        Playground Equipment Needs 147
        Choices and Conflicts 148
        Playgrounds for Every Age and Stage 149
        Caregivers and Playgrounds: Relaxed, Focused, and Involved 150
        Caregivers Enjoy Adult Conversation without Distraction 150
        Going Outdoors: An Orderly Transition 151

9. THE CLASSROOMS 153
    The Infant Nursery 154
        The Importance of Baby's First Year 154
    The Appropriate Nursery: Facilitating the Way Babies Learn 155
        Babies Need to Move 156
        Sounds in the Environment 157
        Learning to Trust 157
        A Good Nursery Is a Calm Place 158
        Sleeping/Waking/Feeding Schedules 159
        Sanitation 159
        Mealtime Routines 160
        Nursery Furnishings and Equipment 161
        How Does This Nursery Make You Feel? 162

  The Toddler Room 162
    The Change in Equipment Meets Toddlers' Changing Needs 162
    How Your Toddler Uses This New Space 163
    Toys and Materials 164
    How Toddlers Use Activity Centers 165
    Cleanup Time with Toddlers 166
    Toddlers' Work 166
    Toddlers and Language 167
    Toddlers' Daily Schedules 167
    Toddlers and Walking 168
    Toddlers and Power 168
  The Terrific Twos 169
    Toddlers and Teenagers 169
    Twos Need Freedom to Try New Things 170
    The Beginnings of Social Interaction 170
    Cleanup Time with Twos 171
    Two-Year-Olds and Language 171
    Respect for Individual Development 172
    Two-Year-Olds and Creative Expression 173
    Learning New Concepts and Names for Things 173
    Music 173
    Developing Attention Spans 174
    The Importance of Pretending 174
    Toilet Training 174
    Activity Centers for Twos 175
    Outdoor Play and Developing Skills 176
  The Preschool Classroom 177
    Preschool Friends 177
    Communication Skills 178
    Competitiveness 178
    "I Can Do It Myself" 178
    Learning Right from Wrong 179
    Imagination, Fantasy, and Reality 179
    The "Why?" Question 180
    Multi-Age versus Single-Age Groupings 180
    Space for Group Time 181
    Preschool Classroom Activity Centers 181

10. THE PEOPLE 187
  The Director 188
    Welcoming You 188
    Helping to Bring out the Best in People 189
    Mercy Mixed with Organization 190
    The Director's Relationship with Children and Parents 191
    The Director's Relationship with Staff 194

    The Caregivers 196
        Staff Qualifications 197
        Saying She Loves Children Isn't Enough...Does She Like Them? 198
        A Teachable Spirit 200
        The Heart of a Servant 200
        Look at the Faces 201
    The Children 202
        At Home in the Environment 202
        Rainy Days 203
        Special Attention 203
    Administrative and Other Staff 204
        Each Person Affects Everyone Else 204
    Vendors and Visitors 205
    Other Parents 205

11. THE SCHEDULES 207
    The Director's Schedule 208
    The Caregivers' Schedules 209
    The Children's Schedules 210
        Alternating Different Types of Activities 211

12. FIELD TRIPS AND EXTRACURRICULAR ACTIVITIES 213
    Field Trips 214
        Logistical Planning 214
        Transportation Methods 215
        Safety First 216
    Extracurricular Activities 217
        What Kinds of Classes Are Offered? 217
        Children Who Don't Participate 217

13. FOOD SERVICE 219
    Meals Provided, Included in Tuition 219
    Who Prepares the Food? 220
    Who Plans the Menus? 220
    Lunch Boxes from Home 220
    Bringing in Breakfast 221
    Special Dietary Needs: Allergies and Religious Requirements 221
    Lunchtime in the Classroom 221
    Giving Thanks 222
    Are Parents Welcome for Lunch? 222

14. EMERGENCY PREPAREDNESS 223
    Preparing Children to Listen 224
    Meeting Firemen and Police Officers 225
    Emergency Drills 225

Meeting Doctors and Nurses 225
Medical Records and Treatment Authorization 226
Natural Disaster 226

PART FIVE

Community–A Pathway to Peace 229

15. Your New Way of Life 231
Your Baby's Adjustment to Day Care 232
Your Toddler's or Preschooler's Adjustment 233
Your Own Adjustment to Day Care 236
    Your Child's Tears Are Different from Your Own 236
    The Child's Orientation to Time 236
Separation Anxiety 237
"What Did You Do at School Today?" 239

16. A Community of Friends 241
Protecting Treasure 242
Fear versus Reason 243
Cultivating Friendships 244
Your Opportunity 245
What Your Child Needs Most 246
Befriending Your Child's Friend 247
Mistakes as a Challenge to Friendship 248
    Life Has Wrinkles 249
    The Unfortunate, Natural Outcome 250
Mercy and Toddlers 252
Mercy and Adults 252
Who Is This Caregiver, and What Does She Really Need? 254
    The Caregiver's Orientation to Time 254
    Little Things Mean a Lot: The Negative Effect 255
    Little Things Mean a Lot: The Positive Effect 255
Kindness Begets Kindness 256
The Power of Mercy 257
When People Show Mercy 258

Chapter Notes 262

INTRODUCTION

I have met countless parents who were looking for peace of mind. They came to me seeking child care services, but they needed much more than that. Child care can be found in any number of places, but finding these services and being confident about using them, well, that is something else altogether.

Child care in America is a controversial subject. There are those who believe that day care is not best for children—and that it can actually be harmful. Therefore, they believe all mothers of preschoolers should stay at home and raise them. Others believe that child rearing while pursuing a fulfilling career is always better than staying at home. These polar opposite positions, and all the opinions in between, add to the strain on ordinary men and women who are trying to raise families and just do what is right. While the debate continues, parents find the best solutions they can, leaving their child at the day care center or family day home in the mornings and going on to work. Many of these working parents hear echoes of the great child care debate resounding every day in their own hearts.

> I HAVE MET COUNTLESS PARENTS WHO WERE LOOKING FOR PEACE OF MIND.

For twenty-seven years, I worked to provide the kind of child day care services for other women's children that I could not find for my own. Soon after establishing and operating a small family day home,

I opened a large child care center for children from birth to five years old in response to overwhelming demand for these services. I worked as the center's director for most of that time and was involved as owner and manager during periods when I employed others in the director position. When Tennessee began rating preschool programs in 2001, my center earned the state's highest star rating (similar to assessments used to rate hotels and restaurants).

It took everything we had—and a lot more—to achieve the warm, child-oriented early learning environment of Creative Learning Center in Nashville. I was blessed with a supportive husband who, among other things, made up for my intermittent budget shortfalls with earnings from his own career. Our two sons recognized the value and importance of this work and made sacrifices, too. We certainly never achieved perfection—sometimes we failed an individual or a family. At times we failed each other. Some years were harder than others. Even so, throughout the life of our center, including the difficult times, the overwhelming majority of the children, parents, and staff were really glad to be there every day. I consider this a kind of miracle.

> FOR TWENTY-SEVEN YEARS, I WORKED TO PROVIDE THE KIND OF CHILD CARE SERVICES FOR OTHER WOMEN'S CHILDREN THAT I COULD NOT FIND FOR MY OWN.

One of the greatest accomplishments of my career was helping parents move from fear and uncertainty to hope and confidence as they placed their little child into the hands of people who were essentially strangers to them. It was a personal joy to help them find the peace of mind they were seeking.

I believe I can help you find peace with your child care solution, too. Not because of anything particularly special about me—far from it. Rather, I believe I can help because I understand what is needed for child care to work well for parents, children, and their caregivers. I've learned the secret to what makes it work so well that seeing real contentment reflected on the faces of both adults and children is the norm. Certain principles and perspectives have a transforming effect when applied to the problem of child care, and they affect young children positively whether initiated by caregivers or by parents.

Peace with Child Care is written for parents of young children, from birth to pre-kindergarten, who need out-of-home child care and are struggling to find it, or who are struggling to live with what they have found. Parents who have a nanny or in-home sitter will discover that many of these principles apply to their child care solution, too. Any parent or grandparent who wants to better understand the young child's developmental needs can benefit from this information.

> THE OVERWHELMING MAJORITY OF PARENTS, CHILDREN, AND CAREGIVERS WERE REALLY GLAD TO BE THERE EVERY DAY.

My perspective on this subject offers some practical benefits to you. As a mother who needed child care services, I have deep empathy for any woman going through such a difficult time. Additionally, as a child care provider, I have had the opportunity to converse with and closely observe hundreds and hundreds of women working their way through the processes you may be experiencing right now. Through both perspectives, I have identified some elements in a mother's search for appropriate child care common to most, if not all, mothers. I'll help you understand how some parents have found resolution to these challenges, while others have continued to wrestle with them for years.

I hope to offer practical help and guidance in several areas. First, through my experiences as a mother, I help you identify exactly why you may be struggling with your emotions at this time. And I help you gain some objectivity about this challenge and give you reality-based encouragement that there is light at the end of this tunnel.

Second, I help you identify your family's real child care need. Reading about and considering these issues will assist you in determining with certainty whether or not you actually have a choice—to find child care at this time or to stay at home with your infant or young child. You will then be able to put this difficult question to rest once and for all.

Third, as a child care provider, I give you inside information about how a good child care center or family day home really works. The phrase "quality child care" has been overused to the point of being almost meaningless. You need to be armed with knowledge about what constitutes true quality, including information on the positive potential inherent in child care as well as some pitfalls. This understanding will better equip you in searching for child care services. If you've already found a center and are dissatisfied, it will enable you to discover exactly why you feel this way as you begin to see what may be missing from your program.

> THE POWER OF THIS INFORMATION IS IN ITS UNIVERSALLY EFFECTIVE PRINCIPLES.

Finally, I will show you effective ways to improve the services you find for your family, in whatever appropriately structured center or family day home you choose. The power of this information is in its universally effective principles. The process of positively influencing your child's day care experience will begin when you start applying them.

Please note that I use certain terms interchangeably, including child care, day care, preschool, and child development program. The information presented here applies to any of them, because the developmental needs of young children in custodial care outside their own homes are the same wherever they are. Any appropriate program for preschoolers will be engaged in child development.

I also use the words caregiver and preschool teacher interchangeably. Just as we recognize that a child's parent truly is his or her first teacher, so it is with caregivers. These providers of direct care have so much influence in children's early lives. Given the way young children learn, their caregivers are indeed their teachers.

Anecdotes in each chapter illustrate the practical application of certain principles. Each is a composite of multiple experiences I had during my years in child care, rather than a factual depiction of a single event. All of the names used are fictitious. While these are fictional illustrations, they nevertheless accurately reflect real life in a child care center.

Most of the adults referenced here—caregivers and parents—are women, so the feminine pronoun is used more often when referring to them. For the sake of clarity, the masculine pronoun is used more often when referring to children.

Over the past several decades, increasing numbers of young children in our nation have been experiencing the influence of significant time spent in the care of persons other than their own families. Because the early years are the most formative in all of life, concerned individuals and groups are investigating what is needed for children to have the best possible outcomes from the day care experience. The subjects of child care and child development are serious and worthy of scholarly and scientific examination.

> MY CENTER WELCOMED FAMILIES OF EVERY RACE, ETHNICITY, AND RELIGIOUS BACKGROUND... THROUGHOUT THOSE YEARS, VIRTUALLY WITHOUT EXCEPTION, EVERY FAMILY FELT AT HOME THERE.

Appropriate standards of professional practice in child care are vitally important to protect young children and to meet their developmental needs, as proven by solid research. I strongly support these standards and the work I've done for most of my adult life reflects this. But I believe that even in those centers that have yet to achieve higher standards of practice, outcomes for young children will be significantly improved when certain principles are applied. This book addresses some of those principles and how they affect the child care environment.

As a Christian, my views on child day care are informed by my faith. And consistent with authentic Christian faith, my center welcomed families of every race, ethnicity, and religious background, including Christian, Jewish, Buddhist, Hindu, Muslim, and those with no religious background at all. Throughout those years, virtually without exception, every family felt at home there.

Our diverse parent group included many upper-middle-class families who could have easily afforded a live-in nanny, as well as families for whom our program presented a significant financial challenge. These parents held many things in common. Above all, they valued having their child in an environment where he or she would be nurtured and receive developmental support, and where his or her individuality was recognized, acknowledged, and truly cherished. What we valued about life in our center was the opportunity to get to know every one of those parents and their children as well as the wonderful staff who worked with us there.

Please don't take offense that I address mothers more than fathers here. I do not consider the father's role less important than the mother's. But for now, let's remember: the person up on that table pushing a little human being out of her body is a woman. And it has been, by far, mostly women who have come to see me about child care.

Christ said, "...and you will know the truth, and the truth will set you free."[1] The freedom that will come from knowing the truth about your individual family's real need is an important key to finding peace with child care.

PART ONE

The Need for Child Care and How Mothers Really Feel About It

1

THE MOTHER'S HEART

As I listened to the distressed voice of the third mother calling that morning to inquire about an opening in the infant nursery, I glanced out the window of the small main-floor work station and saw Jennifer Hawthorne. She was struggling to juggle her diaper bag, which was overflowing with bottles, blankets, infant clothing, a bumper pad and mobile, along with a large unopened package of tiny disposable diapers, and her three-month-old baby girl. All this while wearing an impeccably tailored suit and balanced on four-inch heels. I noted that Betty, one of our caregivers from Nursery I, which was located next to that section of our parking area, had seen Jennifer and was hurrying out to help her.

Jennifer allowed Betty to take the package of diapers but held on to the baby and the bag. This was the first day this new mom would be separated from her child. And on this day she would discover, just like every mom who had done this before her, the heart-wrenching difference between placing your child's name on a child care center's waiting list and placing your child into the hands of someone you really do not know. It was clear to me that this mom was going to have a tough time adjusting to her new way of life.

From the first time I met Jennifer, I knew she was more distressed than the typical new mom enrolling in my child development program. And the typical mom was in pretty serious pain. Over two decades of working with new mothers in the midst of one of the most difficult decisions they would ever have to make had proved this to me. Each of them dealt with the challenge of leaving her baby or young child in day care in her own individual way. Some would make the adjustment more quickly than others. But each of them realized something, on some level, as she drove away from our building and into the world of work: She was leaving behind precious time with her child that could never be recovered. In Jennifer's case, it was going to be quite a while before this beautiful young mother would be able to take a deep breath.

WHAT HAPPENS WHILE YOU'RE MAKING PLANS

If you are a mother seeking child care services for the first time, no one needs to tell you how hard this is. Before the birth, you may have analyzed day care options from every possible angle, placing your unborn child's name on the waiting lists of several good programs. You probably got references from some of their contented clients and assured yourself, "When the time comes, one of the centers will have an available space." You felt in control, ready to return to work after your appointed maternity leave.

On the other hand, perhaps you have been more casual about finding day care. After all, your friends have their children in care and they all seem fine. There are centers everywhere. You're sure you'll find a good spot.

Now your baby is here. And for the first time ever, you have come to a full understanding of the word *precious*. Now you are abiding day and night with a choice so distressing that in many ways it has overwhelmed your life. And it is likely that no one warned you so you could find some way to prepare your heart. I am writing this for you because I believe I can help you find the right situation for your child and can say to you with some authority, It's going to be okay.

SOCIAL ACCEPTABILITY AND PERSONAL ANGUISH

How many times have I witnessed this scene play out? Unlike in the theater where the actors' masks go on, the child care center director's office is where the masks come off. Whether she is a housekeeper or a psychiatrist, a university professor, a sales clerk, or an entrepreneur, one inescapable truth is evident in the majority of women looking for day care: the mother seeking child care services for the first time is in pain.

However composed she may appear or however well prepared she may be to interview the director, as she makes her final decision, something changes. Facing the reality that this is actually going to happen, that her precious treasure will soon be placed into someone else's hands, the voice begins to break and the tears begin to come. Powerful emotions she has kept beneath the surface come pouring out.

Most have the wisdom to just let the feelings wash over them, putting any false sense of dignity aside. The pain of childbirth is small stuff compared to this. My personal experience can best be described as a tearing of the soul, anguish beyond anything I had ever experienced before, including the deaths of people I loved. Because this is a death—the death of a dream of the highest and best kind: the dream of raising your own child.

WHY IS THIS SO HARD?

Not many years ago, there was a lot of shame for parents who chose to use day care. Young couples got the message, sometimes from their own parents, that such a choice was selfish and unwise. In fact, much of the available child care thirty to forty years ago was grossly inadequate. Far too many programs were negligent and dangerous. It was an abysmal situation for children and families in need of help.

Today, more and more child care centers and family day homes have higher standards. Directors and staff have some education or formal training in how children learn and grow. More programs have a supportive developmental curriculum, engaging children in fun, interesting experiences and broadening their understanding of the world, their friends, and themselves. Children in good programs can usually move into the grade-school experience seamlessly. Society accepts day care as a normal part of life now.

> FOR THE FIRST TIME EVER, YOU HAVE COME TO A FULL UNDERSTANDING OF THE WORD PRECIOUS.

Yet, despite the dramatic changes since I first looked for day care in 1970, a mother's experience of loss hasn't changed. Why is that? Why is this still so hard?

THE FUNDAMENTAL PROBLEM

I believe that in their heart of hearts, most women, if not all, really want to be with their child. Something deep within them recognizes how valuable these early years are and how much they will influence who this man- or woman-in-the-making will become. A mother naturally wants to be intimately involved in that process on behalf of her young child.

We see this in nature. The doe stays with the fawn and the robin with her chick until they are ready to face the world on their own. The mom who leaves her child in day care knows he is not ready to face the world alone. Yet she is leaving him in the care of people who are essentially strangers to her. And with limited or no language skills, he is very vulnerable—he has no way to tell her what is happening to him. Finding herself needing to work outside her home, she must now abdicate large blocks of time in an area of her greatest personal influence and desire to someone she doesn't really know. Has she left her little one to face the world alone?

ONE MOTHER'S GREAT EXPECTATIONS

It is natural for a mother to want good things for her child. And we all have experiences and memories that shape our expectations for what we hope our children's lives will be. Here are two of mine.

A Wonderful Memory

It was very dark and quite cold. I couldn't really see the people, but they were all around us, talking with one another in small groups, all moving steadily in the same direction. There seemed to be more and more of them joining us as we walked along. I could feel the excitement and my own sense of wonder and mystery. It was Christmastime, and there was music. Voices singing. Suddenly I was lifted up, up above all of them, and placed on my father's shoulders. I could see their faces now. My daddy and I were part of this large group that had come to see something wonderful. We climbed up a little hill, and then there it was: a huge white Christmas tree with candles all over it. It was glowing with the candlelight and seemed to stretch up to touch the black sky. As I watched and listened, I began to understand what I was seeing. The tree was actually a choir of women and men standing on steps, forming the shape of a tree, wearing white robes, each holding a beautiful candle and singing Christmas carols. This is the earliest memory of my life. I was not yet two and a half years old. It still fills me with joy every time I think of it.

> THERE WAS MUSIC. VOICES SINGING. SUDDENLY I WAS LIFTED UP...

A Painful Memory

The sign in the front yard and the small house beyond looked like they hadn't seen fresh paint for a long time. I felt a squeezing sensation in my chest and wanted to turn around. But the phone directory offered few options for day care, so I drove across the gravel drive, parked, and stepped onto the front stoop.

I could hear a baby crying inside, but no one answered my knock. After several minutes, finding the door unlocked, I let myself in. There was no one there to greet me. The front room was completely empty, except for three infant cribs. One of them contained dirty, crumpled bedding. In another was a small infant, sleeping. In the third crib stood a baby boy around eight months of age. He was naked, except for a cloth diaper so soaked with urine it had fallen down almost to his knees. The skin of the diaper area was covered with a horrible rash. His little red face was wet with tears, and mucus from his nose flowed down into his mouth. The sound of his voice made it clear he had been crying too long. It was a cry of desperation. Voices of women echoed from a room beyond, laughing and talking. I do not know how they didn't hear me come in; it was not possible they didn't hear that child crying.

> I DO NOT KNOW HOW THEY DIDN'T HEAR ME COME IN; IT WAS NOT POSSIBLE THEY DIDN'T HEAR THAT CHILD CRYING.

To say I was shocked by this scene doesn't explain what I felt. My impulse was to pick up the baby and take him out of that awful place, but I realized immediately I couldn't do that. And I was not aware of anything I could do. I fled to my car and drove away, weeping all the way home for that little boy. I vowed my sons would never have to endure a circumstance like that one, but my grief at the reality that some children did was overwhelming.

I am not proud of the fact that I witnessed something so dreadful and took no action. Today I would confront those women, demanding to know how they could neglect an innocent child so flagrantly. I would call the state's child care services department and report in detail to them exactly what I saw. Unfortunately, at that time, the regulatory law and governmental agencies that monitored day care centers were not as advanced as they are today, and their roles were not as well known. At the time, I knew nothing about them. And I never imagined someone in my community would be capable of the behavior I encountered. On that day I didn't know what to do, so I did nothing.

> THE CONTRAST CHANGED ME FOREVER.

The contrast between my personal experience as a young child and the appalling experiences of the children in many of the day care centers I visited while seeking care for my sons changed me forever.

FAMILY LIFE AS IT USED TO BE

Many of us who grew up in the baby boomer generation were fortunate to live in environments where our mothers stayed at home with their children. Obviously, not all American families enjoyed the benefits of such a lifestyle. Just like today, some couples lived in economic conditions that required two incomes to barely subsist. Single-mother families had hardships all their own, and it was entirely up to Mom to provide. Some of those children "took care of" each other. Often, poor families faced challenges the middle class could not have imagined.

Others of us, though, lived in two-parent homes where Mom was able to focus on her family every day. These women spent their time thinking about and planning for the needs of the family as a whole and at times of the needs and wishes of individual family members. When this system was functioning in a healthy way, the refuge from the world a home provided seemed very strong, very significant. Families seemed to have more time to visit and to know each other better. This way of life was quite lovely for everyone, including the women who had this opportunity.

People did not generally look down on homemakers at that time. Most thoughtful people considered this work to be honorable, creative, and important—for the individual family and for society as a whole. Today it appears to be less popular for women to be giving of themselves in this way. I have a different perspective on servanthood.

TWO SERVANTS

I was fortunate to be born into a family where both parents were creative, highly educated people. Among other things, my parents placed great value on all the beauty available for human experience as being a reflection of God. My father was a theologian and pastor. My mother was a musician and educator. They always encouraged their children to stop and take note of beautiful things in nature, in music, in the arts and literature, and in right human relationships. They weren't overbearing in teaching this value. They just enjoyed these things so much that their own experiences flowed naturally into our lives.

> MY PARENTS ALWAYS ENCOURAGED US TO STOP AND TAKE NOTE OF BEAUTIFUL THINGS IN NATURE, IN MUSIC, IN THE ARTS AND LITERATURE, AND IN RIGHT HUMAN RELATIONSHIPS.

My mother did wonderful Martha Stewart-like things for all of us in our home in easy, magical ways, just as her mother had done before her. She was at home with us during our preschool years. At times during that period, she served as minister of music in the church. She led several children's choirs. And the adult choirs she directed performed the great music of the church, including Handel's "Messiah" and Gaul's "The Holy City." Later, after my brothers were in grade school, she worked until retirement with the Board of Education in her county's public school system. She was a classroom teacher for several years and later administered the county's services to special-needs children.

My father always found ways to help meet people's deepest needs, whether he was comforting a family who had suddenly lost a loved one, helping bail an errant member out of jail in the middle of the night, or studying to prepare a sermon. Every year he filled Christmas baskets with modest but meaningful gifts and delivered them to less-fortunate families in our community. Hospital visitation was a routine part of his schedule, as he brought comfort and prayer to the sick and injured who needed their pastor or who were without a pastor and needed someone who cared. For forty years he devoted himself in ministry to the service, salvation, and spiritual development of people. And when he opened his mouth in the pulpit, poetry came out.

Growing up in my parents' home—and within a larger community of folks, most of whom loved and appreciated my parents—was wonderful for me. I look back on all of that now and understand how my great expectations for children's preschool years were formed.

No Perfect Families

Now don't get me wrong. My family was not **perfect. It was** made up of a father, a mother, and their five children—seven flawed people. As the eldest child, I was referred to as "the built-in babysitter." Sometimes my mom was tired, physically and emotionally, from the demands of raising five children, as well as from being "the preacher's wife" and all the expectations that came from a large congregation. Sometimes my father was tense, frustrated, and exhausted—spent, having given all he had to others before he got home to his family.

Times like those were not uncommon in our home, and they weren't so much fun. We live in the

> THERE ARE NO PERFECT FAMILIES, BECAUSE THERE ARE NO PERFECT PEOPLE.

real world. There are no perfect families, because there are no perfect people. This includes the pastor's family and sometimes, especially, the pastor's family.

Just in case you haven't thought about it, I feel I must tell you something. Your family isn't going to be perfect, either. This will be true whether you are able to stay at home with your children or whether you decide that using child care services outside your home is best. But don't despair—provision has been made for this.

2

WHY WE NEED CHILD CARE

After Jennifer Hawthorne began adjusting to our center, she and I found time to get to know each other. She told me that her mother had worked away from home from the time Jennifer was born until she was about three and a half years old. Jennifer remembered hearing her mom talk about how much she regretted missing so much of her early life. A nice neighbor took good care of Jennifer, but her mom always seemed really sad about being away from her during that period. Jennifer's memories of that time were pretty fuzzy.

Jennifer had clear memories, however, of spending time with her mother during the two years before she started kindergarten when they were together every day. She remembered long springtime walks picking wildflowers, reading stacks of children's books on rainy summer afternoons, collecting colored leaves in the fall to decorate the fireplace mantel, and helping her mom bake muffins. There were so many wonderful memories of special times together, and Jennifer longed for the luxury of time like that with her daughter.

PUBLISHED REPORTS ARE AVAILABLE THAT LEND credibility to both sides of the great child care debate and call into question the views of the other side.[1] Whatever your opinion or mine may be about child care in our country, the reality is the use of these services is widespread. I think we can all agree: The tiny child who finds himself in a child care center without his parents should have the best possible day and receive the best possible care—every day. This includes the need for physical safety, developmental support, and, just as certainly, the need for nurture during the most formative years of life.

AMERICA'S WORKFORCE

The National Association of Child Care Resource and Referral Agencies reports that 63 percent of American children under the age of five spend significant time in the care of persons other than their parents.[2]

> WHATEVER YOUR OPINION OR MINE, THE TINY CHILD WHO FINDS HIMSELF IN A CENTER WITHOUT HIS PARENTS SHOULD RECEIVE THE BEST POSSIBLE CARE EVERY DAY.

We see evidence of their mothers' involvement in our nation's workforce everywhere.

More women than men work in the nursing profession to care for us and our families during health crises. These individuals have families, too. Continuing their professional careers requires many nurses who are mothers to seek care for their young children during the workweek. If all nurses, male or female, were to stay at home during the preschool years, the present nursing shortage in our country would look like a picnic by comparison. And in 1999, the Association of American Medical Colleges reported that 50 percent or more of first-year medical students among 40 medical schools were female, an increase they expected to continue.[3] What if half of our physicians were unavailable to us during the first five years of their children's lives?

The medical field is not the only sector of our economy that relies on women to participate in the workforce. How many teachers in grade school, high school, and beyond are female? And increasing numbers of small businesses throughout the U.S. economy are owned by women; in 2002, they represented 28.2 percent of nonfarm companies in the United States.[4] What if they all suddenly decided to suspend their careers to become stay-at-home parents? And what would happen if all female factory workers or retail employees became stay-at-home moms? However anyone feels about women in the workforce, our economy depends upon their participation, and it would grind to a halt without them.

> HOWEVER ANYONE FEELS, OUR ECONOMY DEPENDS ON WOMEN'S PARTICIPATION AND WOULD GRIND TO A HALT WITHOUT THEM.

VERY PERSONAL REASONS

Larger economic reasons are only one aspect of why we need child care in America.

Unfortunately, divorce and separation are tragic and familiar realities for many families. When divorce or abandonment occurs, what is a single mother or father supposed to do? Particularly when child support payments are not made, these parents have no choice but to find the best child care services they can and return to work to put food on the table.

Sometimes illness strikes an intact family, making it impossible for the primary breadwinner to work productively for a season. That parent may be too ill to care for a young child in the home while the spouse is working to make the mortgage payments. Or, an accident can bring permanent disability, changing a family's world as they know it.

Sometimes children are born with profound disabilities. In such circumstances, both parents may need to work to provide for expensive therapies for the disabled child and to pay for the child care of any healthy preschool siblings while no one is at home.

> WHILE I DEEPLY WISH EVERY PARENT COULD BE AT HOME DURING THE PRESCHOOL YEARS, I'VE MET TOO MANY FOR WHOM DAY CARE IS THE ONLY RESPONSIBLE OPTION.

When families confront difficult circumstances like these and have no extended family they can rely on, they don't have the luxury of engaging in debates about the merits or demerits of child care. They just have to find services so they can support themselves and their children. Whatever the studies may say, many of us are fortunate to never personally face the complex realities some families encounter.

While I deeply wish that every parent could be at home with their child during the preschool years, I have met too many in circumstances beyond their control where day care is the only responsible option.

OTHER FINANCIAL REASONS

Taxes

According to The Tax Foundation, a nonpartisan tax research group based in Washington, D.C., the cumulative federal, state and local tax burden in 2006 came to 31.6 percent of the average U.S. family's income.[5] This reportedly represents a larger share of the average family's gross household income than food, clothing and housing, combined.[6] Is it any wonder many families feel they need a dual income?

Housing costs

Owning your own home has always been an important part of the American Dream. While home ownership is at its highest levels ever, many of these dreams have been purchased with nontraditional mortgages. Some families live with the pressure that their dream home may become a nightmare once interest rates rise, particularly if their unconventional home loan was for a bigger house than they could otherwise afford.[7]

Health care costs

Despite the fact that we are the wealthiest nation in the world, the number of people in our population struggling with illness is increasing, driving up medical costs. These costs impact families' health insurance premiums.[8] Many families need dual incomes just to pay for health insurance.

Life versus lifestyle—my personal mistake

Unwise financial decisions are a snare for many couples today. And for many single working parents, one wrong financial turn can add to their already overwhelming burden. Advertisers conspire to make us feel inadequate if we don't have the best of everything. We are constantly told that we deserve this or that, and it's easy to lose sight of the importance of making wise financial decisions. In this section, I'll use my own personal mistake as an example of how this can happen.

> IT'S EASY TO LOSE SIGHT OF THE IMPORTANCE OF MAKING WISE FINANCIAL DECISIONS.

My family's problem began with a practical, legitimate need. My husband was in the Marine Corps during the Vietnam era. We lived in officer housing on base that was infested with earwigs—small, shiny insects with lobsterlike pincers. Our sons were born during this period, and I was continually worried that one of these creatures might pinch one of our babies. Thankfully, it never happened. But living with that fear, in addition to all the general fears of wartime, had a big impact on me and my thoughts about home.

When we left the military, I wanted an insect-free zone for our sons, and my husband agreed. If we had searched with greater determination, we might have found several suitable options. But by paying "just a little more," we were able to lease a brand-new townhouse in an upscale part of our city. No earwigs there! My husband was employed by one of the large, multinational accounting firms, and as a young CPA, his future looked very bright. But we soon realized that "just a little more" was far too much, and we couldn't wait for that bright future to arrive—I had to go to work to help make ends meet.

> WE SOON REALIZED THAT "JUST A LITTLE MORE" WAS FAR TOO MUCH.

This unexpected change in our family's life and the search for care for my two little boys, including everything I saw and learned in that difficult process, is why I devoted much of my life to providing child care services. As I look back on our choice for better housing in 1970, I realize that if I were faced with the same circumstances today, my decision would be quite different.

You can see how one seemingly innocuous choice can have such a lasting impact on a family. Meeting many parents as a child care provider over almost three decades convinced me that while this is certainly not relevant for some, unwise financial decisions predispose many others to needing child care services. If using child care is an unintended consequence of taking a financial risk, the most valuable aspects of a family's quality of life can become diminished by their "improved" lifestyle.

3

WHY YOU NEED CHILD CARE

Dan and Mary Ellen Duckworth moved to Nashville from South Georgia. Dan had just taken a job with a prominent law firm, and Mary Ellen had landed a good job with a large bank. Their future looked full of promise. Unfortunately, they were already living the lifestyle they hoped to afford one day, including the upscale neighborhood, the big cars, and all the trappings of success.

The Duckworths were a friendly, outgoing couple, and it was fun to be around them. Still, I could tell something was bothering Mary Ellen. In time, she told me her story.

When Mary Ellen was a young child, her parents owned and operated a very successful small business in their town. The business consumed almost all their time. So throughout her childhood, Mary Ellen spent more time with her grandmother than with her mother. She and her nana were very close, but Mary Ellen missed her mother.

Dan and Mary Ellen met in college and married right after he graduated from law school. By their first anniversary, Mary Ellen had completed her degree and a baby boy was on the way. When Patrick was born, she wanted more than anything to just be with her child. She expected to stay at home with Patrick until he entered kindergarten, when she planned to put her business degree to work. Mary Ellen was following through with her plan until Dan won his first big case. After that, he received an offer he couldn't refuse from the large Nashville firm. So here they were.

For reasons she couldn't understand, Dan's priorities seemed to change after that big win. He was the one pushing for the luxury home and expensive lifestyle. Mary Ellen felt uneasy about it, but it was hard to say no to a beautiful new house. Dan and Mary Ellen soon realized that their finances were out of control. She would have to go to work and put twenty-month-old Patrick in day care.

CLEARLY, CHILD DAY CARE HAS BECOME VERY IMPORTANT to many families in our country. Now I hope you will take a critical look at why your family needs child care. There are some hard things in this chapter, but there is no promise that bits and pieces of truth will make us free. The promise is that "the truth will make you free." If you want to experience real peace with your child care decision, you really must confront the truth about why your family needs these services. What is revealed in doing so will be vital to your ability to come to terms with your choice and move beyond any sense of loss or grief you may be experiencing now.

> IF YOU WANT REAL PEACE WITH YOUR CHILD CARE DECISION, CONFRONT THE TRUTH ABOUT WHY YOUR FAMILY NEEDS THESE SERVICES.

EVALUATING DREAMS

Dreaming is important to all of us. Our hopes and dreams can motivate us to think about what we want to accomplish in life. Then we can set goals for ourselves, using determination and discipline to work toward and reach them.

Sometimes, though, we have unrealistic dreams. Some may be fleeting wishes or thoughts that we know will never be. At other times, we may hold tightly to an unrealistic dream. This can happen when we experience something that leaves us with feelings we need to resolve so we don't end up hindering our real life.

For example, you may relate to what was once a passing wish for me. Remember falling in love? When you first met the man who would become the father of your child, you may have felt, as I did, that you had no need for anything more than his presence. I would have been content to live with him on a deserted island, playing on the beach and catching fish for dinner!

> THERE IS NO PROMISE THAT BITS AND PIECES OF TRUTH WILL MAKE US FREE.

After forty years of marriage, I'm still in love with that man, and we are living a wonderful life. But we're not alone on an island somewhere. We have family and friends and work we love. And we wouldn't change any of it, even though our real life is much more complicated and involves a lot more responsibility than the island life I sometimes envisioned. Just like your life, this is how it is in the grown-up world.

REAL LIFE IN THE GROWN-UP WORLD

Maybe you intended to stay home with your children until they entered grade school—or at least for the first year or two, or the first six months. Now, circumstances make that impossible. Like Dan and Mary Ellen Duckworth, or my husband and me, your financial commitments may be leading you back to work before you planned.

Or you may be a teacher with a wonderful surprise pregnancy coupled with a classroom full of children who are depending on you to finish what you started in their first year of school. Or, perhaps you're a medical professional who must return to work after maternity leave because you are the only practitioner of your specialty in the community.

Maybe you work in a department store, and while your salary is not high, it is such an important part of your family budget that you can't imagine how you and your husband could do without it. Or you may be in an even more difficult position: the marriage you thought was coming did not work out, and now you are feeling quite alone, facing loss upon loss.

A DECISION ONLY YOU CAN MAKE

Whatever led you to consider child care is between you and your spouse. Or, if you are a single parent, then it is your business alone. No one has enough information to second-guess your best judgment about this. There may be people in your life whose opinions you value who are insistent about this decision one way or the other. While it is wise to invite counsel from people you respect, the key issue is your own opinion of what you are going to do.

> LOOK CRITICALLY AT YOUR FAMILY'S TRUE NEEDS.

Before you can be at peace with yourself about this, you're going to have to look critically at your family's needs. If after this evaluation you determine that going back to work is best for you, then you will be able to accept and live with this decision. You will know it is the best choice at this time for you, your spouse, and your child.

UNRESOLVED FEELINGS AND UNREALISTIC DREAMS

Everyone has been hurt by someone else, sometimes deeply. When that happens to us, it is natural to respond emotionally. This may involve feelings of sorrow and loss, betrayal, mistrust, or anger. But if we allow ourselves to be overcome by these normal, negative emotions, we may make some very bad decisions. We are all vulnerable in this way because we're human. And it takes courage and maturity to face aspects of our lives that we would prefer to avoid. But the freedom we gain by addressing unresolved feelings in life is more than worth the effort.

What does this have to do with day care? Maybe nothing in your case. But in my observations of families as a child care provider, I firmly believe unresolved emotional issues can be a relevant and even motivating factor for some parents, as it clearly was for the Duckworths. Mary Ellen told me that as she and Dan began to discuss the problems with their finances, he confessed that his father's inappropriate attitudes caused Dan to feel he had to prove himself and his personal worth. That was a significant part of what was driving his unrealistic financial choices. One by one, unwise financial decisions forced this couple to a lifestyle change they hadn't planned on—putting Patrick into child care at a time they would never have chosen to do so.

> DECIDING TO PLACE YOUR CHILD INTO THE HANDS OF SOMEONE YOU DO NOT KNOW IS AS SERIOUS AS ANY DECISION YOU WILL EVER HAVE TO MAKE.

This dynamic may not be relevant for your family, but in your search for peace with child care, at the very least it is worth looking at. Deciding to place your child into the hands of someone you do not know during his or her most formative years is as serious as any decision you will ever have to make. How you proceed may have ramifications that will echo in your family's life for years. So if you are a person of faith, now is the time to pray—for wisdom and strength, and for clarity to recognize any issue that could cloud your judgment. Many, many people benefit by seeking strength and resources from beyond themselves, and I have found no better way to do this than through prayer.

THE DECISION TO STAY AT HOME

Only you can decide your budgetary priorities and define what is necessary. If you don't have a family budget, please sit down and make one. This is one of the most important steps you can take before going any further. If you don't know where to begin, let me recommend Dave Ramsey's nationally syndicated radio program, "The Dave Ramsey Show".[1] Dave's book *Financial Peace* is available everywhere.

After carefully analyzing your family's true needs, you may discover that your family has fallen into the advertisers' trap, as have many other families. You may be spending more than you need to spend on things that don't matter to you nearly as much as the little person napping in the next room.

> YOU MAY BE SPENDING MORE THAN YOU NEED TO SPEND ON THINGS THAT DON'T MATTER TO YOU NEARLY AS MUCH AS THE LITTLE PERSON NAPPING IN THE NEXT ROOM.

If that is the case, I urge you to reconsider using child care at this time. Hold a garage sale, Dave Ramsey-style, in order to get rid of some of those less-important things. Selling your home and buying a smaller one, or just paying the fee to break a lease, would not be a radical choice if it allows you to have your child at home with you.

Many couples have made financial decisions influenced by their concern for what the neighbors or their friends or family thought about their lifestyle. Such decisions can result in unnecessary and irreplaceable loss. If you're a young couple, a few years of a reduced lifestyle may seem like an eternity, but I promise you, it will pass quickly.

If you are deeply unhappy about using child care services, is it possible you might stay home for a period of time and continue your career later? Your employer or human resources staff has likely encountered workers so consistently distracted by such family concerns that productivity suffered greatly. In fact, your HR staff may have direct experience with scrambling to find a replacement for an otherwise fine employee who abruptly left precisely because of an inability to find a suitable day care arrangement. Your company is not likely to be enthusiastic about the idea of an extended unpaid leave of absence for you. They may not be willing or able to grant you one. Therefore, you should have a strong sense of your company's Work/Life policies before you have such a candid conversation. If their decision turns out favorably for you, it is probably because by not burning bridges with you now they may save many thousands of dollars in recruitment costs later.

If it is right for your family that you stay at home rather than return to work, you will probably have to sacrifice certain things, and your child will, too. Birthday parties may not be as large or as fancy. You may not be able to buy all the cute designer clothes you'd love to see your child wearing. But birthdays come only once a year. The mom who stays home has the luxury of time to celebrate being with her child every day. And it's amazing how fast children outgrow expensive clothes.

Look around you. Many of the people you know and many of the strangers you see at the mall and on the streets have fallen for a lie. Many seek happiness by acquiring more and more material things, while their marriage and family relationships become more and more impoverished. An expensive car and granite countertops can never compare to the value of this time with your child. Besides, if they're still important to you several years from now, you can always buy them later. The treasures you will gather while staying home with your child will last forever.

> IF YOU ARE DEEPLY UNHAPPY ABOUT USING CHILD CARE SERVICES, IS IT POSSIBLE YOU MIGHT STAY HOME FOR A PERIOD OF TIME AND CONTINUE YOUR CAREER LATER?

Counting the cost

For many families, the benefits of a second income end up being much less than they expected. As you examine your budget, please look realistically at the following costs, some of which you may not have considered. You may think of others:

- Child care tuition and annual fees
- Fees for extracurricular activities at your child's center: dance, swim, computer classes, etc.
- A second car and all the fuel, insurance, and maintenance costs associated with its use
- Parking
- A business wardrobe
- Dry cleaning
- Meals out when you're too tired to shop and cook
- Income and social security taxes' effects on your take-home pay
- Effects on long-term goals

After analyzing everything, you may discover that by making certain sacrifices, you can stay home with your child. If you recognize this is your heart's desire and what is best for you and your family, know that it won't be easy. Often that which is truly worthwhile is not easy. But choosing what is best for your family is always, well, best.

If you have decided to stay home, please continue reading, because there are numerous portions of this book relevant to life at home with your child. These truths would have made my life as a young mother much easier if I had understood then what I understand now.

THE DECISION TO USE CHILD CARE SERVICES

Your evaluation of your family's finances may have led you to the opposite conclusion. After selecting and applying the right budgetary plan, you may decide it is necessary for you to go back to work to avoid serious financial hardship. Or you may have compelling career obligations that you simply cannot ignore, because your work affects the livelihood or well-being of many other families. If you believe that you really have no other choice, then the right thing for you at this time may indeed be a return to work. This may be the very best thing for your family, and that includes your child.

True guilt versus false guilt

If choosing child care is the best answer for your family, then there is no need to be plagued by guilt. Let me explain what I mean.

There are two different kinds of guilt—true guilt and false guilt. The first kind comes from your own conscience, that spiritual thing built into your heart that enables you to discern right from wrong. True guilt is a good thing, because it signals that something bad has happened or is about to.

When a jury finds a person guilty of a crime, he usually is truly guilty. If he feels guilt or remorse for what he has done, this is a good thing. Progress is made as the wrongdoer begins to think differently about the deed he has done and the attitude that allowed him to make such a choice.

> IF USING CHILD CARE IS RIGHT FOR YOUR FAMILY, THEN THERE'S NO NEED TO BE PLAGUED BY GUILT. LET ME EXPLAIN...

The purpose of true guilt is to help us find and choose right, versus finding and choosing wrong. Deliberately tuning out our conscience over a long period of time can alter our ability to hear and respond to it. But the fact that you are reading this book indicates your conscience is serving you and your family well. If choosing child care is right for your family, there is no need to ever feel guilty about it.

False guilt originates from a different source than true guilt. It is not a good thing. False guilt is that voice in your head beating you up with blame and condemnation. It can be relentless and corrosive to the soul. The fact is, we all experience false guilt at certain times in our lives. And you will probably experience false guilt while your child is in day care. It helps to stop and analyze what you're feeling so you can recognize what is true and what is false.

Grief

It is important to distinguish between grief and guilt. Both can make you feel awful, but they are different. Grief comes when we lose something or someone deeply important to us. Placing your child in day care—even if it is the very best center in the world—will involve grief. That's because you know you are losing precious opportunities and experiences with your child that can never be replaced. It will be inexpressibly difficult to do this. But if child care is right for you, you will work through this grief much faster than you would if you were using these services when it was not right for your family but you did it anyway.

> PLACING YOUR CHILD IN DAY CARE—EVEN IF IT IS THE VERY BEST CENTER IN THE WORLD—WILL INVOLVE GRIEF.

One of my favorite scriptures in the Bible is in the Old Testament, recording the promise of God that He will restore the years locusts have eaten. We all need this promise. We've all had years—sometimes many years—that involved great personal loss. God has ways of restoring our lives that go far beyond what we could ask for, or even imagine.

IF IT'S BEST FOR YOUR FAMILY, IT'S BEST FOR YOUR CHILD

Let me restate something that is very important. If choosing child care is right for you and your family, then this choice encompasses what is best, at this time, for your child. When you receive this truth into your heart, it will be liberating in several ways. First, acknowledging what is best for your family helps you remain conscious of the big picture. As you focus on this bigger vision, you gain confidence and a sense of purpose in your day-to-day life. This new self-assurance gives you strength and enables you to persevere.

Additionally, you will be able to accept that real life will happen to your child in day care, just as it does at home. Your child has both good and difficult days at home, and so it will be in the center. This is how life works for everyone, and this is normal.

It is natural to want everything to always be sweetness and light for your little one, but you know that isn't realistic. If we are honest with ourselves, we have to admit that often it is the harder things in life that help us grow into stronger adults. And while young children need protection from issues that are beyond their capacity to handle, they, too, grow and mature through developmentally appropriate challenges. Learning to walk involves some falling.

> CONFIDENCE IN YOUR DECISION GIVES CONFIDENCE TO YOUR CHILD.

Real life happens to all children, wherever they are. Understanding this will give you a better, more realistic perspective when your child faces some difficulty at the center, as he or she inevitably will. You won't be as likely to feel it's all your fault or that you're a bad parent—that you should never have left your child in day care in the first place. You're not as likely to become confused or think you've done something wrong, when in fact you are doing exactly what is right for your family.

The parent who continues to agonize over whether or not she is doing the right thing unwittingly forces her child to participate. Parents struggling with guilt reflect this uncertainty and sorrow to their child in some way every day. This child experiences the parent's endless rehashing of this basic family life issue. The parent's ongoing conflict diminishes the child's ability to adjust to day care.

On the other hand, having confidence in your decision gives confidence to your child. The child of such a parent knows the day care center is where he belongs while Mom is at work. He becomes entirely comfortable with that and is free to enjoy the day care experience.

After considering the issues we've addressed, if you decide that child care is right for your family, go forward with confidence, hope and joy. I am going to show you principles that can make it work wonderfully for you and your child.

PART TWO

What the Young Child Really Needs and How to Find It

4

WHO IS THIS DEVELOPING CHILD

(AND WHAT DOES HE REALLY NEED)?

ack was a healthy, happy two-year-old boy with dark hair and big brown eyes. He looked out at his world as if it were a great big party, planned just for him. Sam and Gina had decided to enroll Zack in day care when he turned two. Zack had started talking more and more lately, and although his grandparents couldn't understand a word of it, his parents thought they knew what he was saying most of the time. There was never a question that Zack would be in day care. Everyone Sam and Gina knew had their children in day care.

Zack was an active boy, and Sam and Gina knew if they found a center he liked, he would be fine. He'd just play with his little friends all day. So they chose three centers, each located at a comfortable distance between their home and workplaces, and scheduled the tours.

Sam and Gina's plan while touring the programs was to just watch Zack very closely to see which one he seemed most comfortable with. His reaction to the other children and how he liked the classrooms and the playgrounds—especially the playgrounds—would be their signal. They were confident Zack would let them know, in his own way, what was best for him.

Zack fell in love with the playground of the center that happened to be the most convenient for them. The staff members seemed nice, and all the children seemed to be playing well, so they enrolled him on the spot. On his first day, Zack cried when they started to leave but was quickly distracted when he looked out the window and saw the railroad-engine rocker. Zack loved trains. When Sam and Gina arrived to pick up Zack that afternoon, the teacher told them that he had done fine for a first day. And there he was out on the playground with that red engine, rocking away.

As the days passed, however, Zack seemed to be having a harder time saying good-bye in the mornings. This was the opposite of what Gina and Sam had expected. They began noticing some other things, too—things that left them feeling increasingly uncomfortable. Although the adult/child ratios were fine on the day of their tour, now more children had joined the class, and Zack's teacher didn't seem as relaxed and friendly.

On the day of their tour, Sam and Gina had had their mind on Zack. They watched him carefully as he toddled from here to there, obviously delighted with having a new place to play. They hadn't really looked too closely at a lot of things about this center, because their focus had been entirely on their child.

FIRST THINGS FIRST—YOUR CHILD'S DEVELOPMENTAL NEEDS

There are certain practical considerations you must address as you search for the right child care center. Some of these include the program's hours of operation, the ages of children served, whether tuition is within your range, and convenience of location. All of these are important issues to think about. If it's going to work, the program must meet your needs in practical ways.

But let's remember to put first things first. Your child is the person who will be spending so much time at day care, so finding a center that meets your personal needs for convenience and comfort, while very important, must not be your first priority. This program must meet your child's developmental needs. Failure to assure yourself of this will inevitably result in a lack of peace.

HAVE I FOUND THE RIGHT CENTER IF HE LIKES IT?

I have met several parents who, in attempting to assure themselves of this important aspect of care, mistakenly believed they could base their entire decision on which center their child liked best.

When I met Sam and Gina, they had realized what a big mistake they made enrolling their child into a day care that they discovered had serious organizational flaws. Unfortunately, they never thought about how a good program was set up until they found themselves and their child in one that was poorly structured.

This couple was totally devoted to their little boy, but Zack's essentially happy disposition—a real blessing—set them up for their error. Because he was such a cheerful, contented child, his parents had never felt the need to find out more about how young children learn and grow. Zack was obviously doing fine at home, so his parents made some unrealistic assumptions about his needs at day care. They failed to educate themselves about what life in the center with a group of other children would be like for Zack.

THE NATURE OF THIS DECISION

Deciding which center your child will attend is not like choosing a car or the location of your wedding ceremony. This decision carries much greater significance, because it will impact future happiness, well-being, and quality of life. It isn't realistic to expect a little child to help you make this big choice.

What you do now will call upon your very best judgment in order to choose wisely. You are deciding the nature and quality of influences that will affect most of the waking hours of your child's preschool years, the most formative in all of life. After you make the right choice and your child is effectively integrated into the program, he will confirm your decision through his enthusiasm for going to school. He'll be happy to go most mornings. He may even be reluctant to leave in the afternoon at times. And you will continually recognize the remarkable changes in your child's development that bring him new friends, increased curiosity, joy in learning, increasing self-control and self-confidence, and a healthy pride in his abilities and accomplishments.

THE NATURE OF THE YOUNG CHILD

Long before there were preschools, day care programs, or child development centers, young children were learning and developing. Whether in the most primitive cultures or the most technologically advanced, the young child's nature is to learn and grow.

> THE QUESTION IS NOT WHETHER YOUR CHILD WILL BE LEARNING IN DAY CARE, BUT WHAT HE WILL BE LEARNING.

Except in circumstances of severe illness or disability, all young children learn to walk, talk, interact with others, and ultimately grow to adulthood. As adults, they become capable of providing for themselves and their own children. This really is a remarkable transformation. The fact is, even people whose early years are spent in the simplest cultures may choose to alter their way of life by acquiring formal education, sometimes requiring them to relocate and learn a new language.

Therefore, the question is not whether your child will be learning in his preschool years, but what he will be learning. And this is why your day care choice is so important.

HOW CAN I KNOW WHAT TO LOOK FOR?

Some of the things children learn will have a very positive impact on their future, while other experiences can have the opposite effect. Some children spend their preschool years in homes that strengthen self-esteem and encourage them to become the best they can be. Other children face neglect, fear, and even abuse on a regular basis. In whatever circumstance the young child finds himself, he is learning continuously.

Clearly, children who grow up with hopeful, positive influences have a distinct advantage over the child who is abused. All early experiences, whether positive or negative, have the potential to form vivid memories that can affect a person throughout his or her life.

Just as there is wide disparity in the homes children grow up in, there is disparity in the quality of experiences children have in day care. Your child care solution will fall somewhere between your dream program where everything works perfectly for every child every day, and the uninspired, lifeless program staffed by people who have no vision or heart for their work. Given such a broad range in quality of care, what is really important? What should you look for?

Before parents can know what they need to be looking for, they need to have a realistic understanding of who the developing child really is. First, let's think about who he is not.

WHO THE CHILD IS NOT

Margaret Mahler, a Hungarian child psychologist studying human development, concluded that an infant doesn't know at first that he and his mother are two separate persons.[1] Obviously, over time, it's important for a baby to come to understand this.

Similarly, it is important for parents to understand and accept that their child is not part of who they are in the way that, say, their hand is or that their house or their careers are. We do not possess our children. Children are their own persons, however tiny they may be. From the very beginning, a child is a human being in the process of becoming an individual adult, with individual rights and responsibilities. Our rights and responsibilities as their parents include, among others, those of guidance, provision, and governance.

> CHILDREN ARE THEIR OWN PERSONS, HOWEVER TINY THEY MAY BE.

AN ADULT-IN-THE-MAKING

As parents, we hope to one day stand on even ground with our adult child and have this person in some way tell us they recognize and appreciate all our love and sacrifice. I believe if that is to happen in the way we hope, we must remember to view even the youngest human as an adult-in-the-making. Parents and caregivers who have this perspective toward the child recognize and appreciate what he or she is accomplishing in life right now, every day.

Segments of the automobile industry have taught us to appreciate powerful automobiles that go from zero to sixty miles per hour in five or six seconds. Building engines capable of that is quite an accomplishment. But your baby's progress is even more impressive. Part of why he manages such astonishing growth and development in these early years is that he possesses a kind of courage and persistence—a willingness to try and fail and try and try again.

The child whose parents and caregivers recognize and respect this reality is distinctly blessed. Responsive parents and caregivers who commit themselves to the child's well-being and who are there for him to notice and support his achievements can have a permanent powerful influence for good in his life.

HE NEEDS TO LEARN HOW TO LEARN

When we visit a public library and see many large rooms filled with countless books, it is humbling to recognize the vast stores of knowledge contained in them. And the more we learn, the more we understand how little we know in the great scheme of things. No single person, no matter how intellectually gifted she may be, can possess all the knowledge available to her. Rather, we learn the things we are drawn to by our natural gifts, talents, and interests.

The actual facts your child will learn at day care are less important than his more significant work at this time in his life: learning how to learn. Whether at home with parents or in out-of-home day care, when a child enters an environment that demonstrates learning as an exciting, fulfilling, and limitless process, he or she will naturally want more. This is why children who have had a positive preschool experience are excited and joyously expectant about entering grade school. They want more of what they've already experienced. This gives them a big head start in their education. And this is one important component in what a good preschool experience will provide. It is imperative for you to understand what appropriate developmental support is in all areas of your child's development.

APPROPRIATE DEVELOPMENTAL SUPPORT

Your young child is simultaneously growing and developing in many different ways. Each child's rate of development in each area is unique, and development in the various areas is interconnected. For example, it would be a big mistake for a program to focus on children's cognitive development while failing to support development of motor skills. Learning concepts while seated at a desk is not the right approach for preschoolers, because the young child's thinking and knowing self develops naturally as he touches, explores, and manipulates objects. The development of his fine motor skills, the muscles of the fingers and hands, facilitates intellectual growth. The staff of a good child development program understands and respects the way this happens and will avoid tampering with this amazing natural process.

Good preschool teachers encourage young children to learn and discover new things, but they don't pressure children to perform. Young children do not have the emotional framework for that kind of pressure, which could damage their natural enthusiasm for learning, possibly impeding their later success in grade school. Rather, preschool teachers support and encourage children as they explore and discover, motivated by their innate curiosity. They offer materials, equipment, and activities that are appealing and fun for children, supporting development in the various areas of growth.

He needs to develop language

In a good center, children hear a lot of conversation throughout the day. They hear their teachers talking with one another as well as with their own parents and other adults in friendly, respectful ways. And they hear teachers speaking with other children. In this interactive environment, children develop positive expectations of social discourse. As this kind of interaction is modeled for them, they're encouraged more and more to use language to resolve problems and to elicit the support of friends to reach goals. They also try out their developing language skills through pretending play, both on the playground and in their activity centers.

Caregivers read to children often. They use high-quality books with stories that fascinate and capture the imagination and the emotions. These books are often accompanied by spectacular artwork that is accessible and appealing to the young child. A good program will always be seeking new books for their collection. And teachers take advantage of offerings by public libraries. Often, librarians will select a large group of books for caregivers to check out all at once to supplement a center's private library.

When caregivers talk with children, they frequently get down on the child's eye level for good one-on-one conversation. Teachers are not only quick to respond to a child's questions, but also ask many open-ended questions of children in their care. Some examples would be, "What would you like to do on this rainy day?" or "Look, Sarah, Johnny is missing his mommy this morning. What can we do to help him feel better?" Listening and responding to questions like these encourages children to reason things through. Teachers enhance language development and cognitive skills by finding such opportunities to lead children beyond yes or no answers.

> THE STAFF OF A GOOD CHILD DEVELOPMENT PROGRAM UNDERSTANDS AND RESPECTS THE WAY LEARNING HAPPENS.

HE NEEDS SOCIAL AND EMOTIONAL DEVELOPMENT

Preschool teachers help young children learn the give-and-take of social interaction—how to get along with one another and begin making friends. And a good caregiver naturally becomes one of your child's true friends—a source of reliable support, encouragement, and protection.

The ability to form cooperative, mutually respectful relationships is important in families, as well as in business and social life. It makes sense that when a child begins to consider the needs of others and experiences friendship early in life, it will be easier to form successful relationships later. An adult with great potential for success but who is unable to involve others in his work will not succeed in the way he might if he had better people skills. Most endeavors require the ability to lead at times, and the person with poorly developed social skills is at a big disadvantage.

Helping children develop socially should be one of the most significant goals of any center. Teachers help in this area by involving preschoolers in projects that require cooperation, such as painting a mural welcoming parents and grandparents to the annual picnic. When several artists are involved in the effort and teachers are close by to help the process along, children learn ways to solve problems together and resolve conflicts.

> THE CHILD WHO IS BEGINNING TO UNDERSTAND HOW TO GET ALONG WITH OTHERS IS ALSO BEGINNING TO DEVELOP EMOTIONAL CONTROL.

Home and block centers, which often facilitate pretending play, are another good way for children to learn kindness, sharing, and self-control. Trained, attentive staff recognize when to allow conflict resolution to go forward without their help and when to intervene. At the appropriate time they will be ready with suggestions for words or sentences the struggling child may use such as, "May I play with it when you're through?" or "Please help me put the trucks away."

The child who is beginning to understand how to get along with others is also beginning to develop emotional control. He recognizes that the fun of cooperative play has a price. He must think about and consider other people's desires and feelings. Failure to do so can lead to some unpleasantness. So instead of screaming or lashing out at our friends, we must stop and think of other ways to work out problems. These are important life lessons, and the child in a quality program has lots of opportunities, along with appropriate adult support, to begin to understand how friendship works.

He needs pre-academic skills

There are some fundamental pre-academic skills any young child can learn in fun ways, whether directed by a preschool teacher or by a parent. These skills prepare him to more easily understand the information that kindergarten and grade school teachers will provide. As with many kinds of learning, foundations and building blocks of knowledge must be in place before other information can be understood.

Children in a healthy home learn many skills with pre-academic value through day-to-day activities with Mom or Dad—for example, unloading the clothes dryer and sorting, folding, and putting clothes away; unloading groceries, placing one box of spaghetti on the counter and putting the other two boxes in the pantry; baking cookies, including all the measuring, pouring, and clock-watching this requires; weeding flower beds, discriminating between weeds and seedling flowers.

Children in a good child care center also learn pre-academic skills naturally as they explore the materials and equipment in their environment. Sometimes, though, their teachers take a more methodical approach to teaching certain skills. An example of an important pre-academic skill is learning left-to-right progression. Certain games and equipment for young children help them develop an expectation that some things flow from left to right. This is a readiness skill that helps prepare children for reading, and, interestingly, it is supported by certain motor-skills development.

You and I understand that there is a left and a right, and when we read, we don't have to think about it. But for your young child, spatial awareness and improving muscular control are precursors to establishing left-to-right progression as a pre-academic skill. After all, left and right on the page will not make sense until the child knows to distinguish between one place and another by his own experience.

Another example of a pre-academic skill is one that helps prepare a child for basic arithmetic. Learning number concepts is distinct from counting from one to ten by rote memorization. Through various games and manipulative materials, the child learns what one or two or six really means, by causing and experiencing such numerical differences. He will then be able to respond correctly when his teacher asks him to place four cups and four napkins on the table at lunchtime.

> BUILDING BLOCKS OF KNOWLEDGE MUST BE IN PLACE BEFORE OTHER INFORMATION CAN BE UNDERSTOOD.

HE NEEDS TO DEVELOP MOTOR SKILLS

We all recognize that young children spend much of their time on the move. Unless they are ill or disabled, this is a universal characteristic. Through this almost constant motion, children develop strength, coordination, and control of their muscles. Centers not only accommodate freedom of movement through the physical arrangement of classrooms and playgrounds, but also encourage it with certain planned, teacher-directed activities.

Caregivers in a good program will not use a crib or infant swing as a child management tool for their own convenience. Playpens take up critical floor space needed for scooting and crawling and will not be used at all. A baby's freedom of movement is vitally important across a range of developmental areas. And when parents or teachers constrain infants by holding them too much or by requiring inordinate time in a crib or swing, normal development can be delayed.

Older preschoolers are not expected to be quiet and still in their class too much. They have freedom to move around the room and make appropriate choices for themselves. Centers provide outdoor space to support an older child's large muscle, or gross motor, skills development in a variety of ways, including offering different types of playground equipment. Follow-the-leader games, dance, and gymnastics indoors also enhance large muscle strength and control.

Fine motor skills develop as children manipulate art materials, place pegs into a pegboard, put books back onto the bookshelf, and so forth. You can see how the important development of eye-hand coordination is strengthened by these activities as well.

HE NEEDS CREATIVE EXPRESSION

Typically developing preschool children are entirely uninhibited about making art. When allowed opportunities to explore the arts in an environment that provides appropriate support and encouragement, they naturally approach these experiences with a great sense of freedom, competency, and joy.

All young children can draw or paint, sing, dance, make up a story, or act in a brief play with wonderful effectiveness. Parents and teachers enhance this capacity when they avoid passing any judgment that could cause a child to become embarrassed or uncertain of his or her ability.

When child development programs include the arts, everyone can learn to appreciate the validity of children's individual artistic ideas. This gives each child confidence that extends to other areas. Some children have

> THE UNSTRUCTURED PURSUIT OF ARTISTIC EXPRESSION OFFERS WIDE-RANGING SUPPORT TO THE CHILD'S DEVELOPMENT.

natural talents in the arts, but every child benefits through participation, especially when adults express true enjoyment of children's personal creations.

Sometimes people develop inhibition toward artistic pursuits and unwittingly communicate their ideas about art in ways that stifle rather than foster creative learning. Parents or teachers may inadvertently pass along their personal feelings of reluctance or inadequacy toward artistic pursuits as they view the artwork of children by saying, for example, "You're not big enough to paint yet." This statement reveals the adult's negative judgment of the child's art, which could cause this child to be reluctant to paint again. Parents and teachers can prevent or forestall such a loss by promoting the unstructured pursuit of artistic expression, which offers wide-ranging support to the child's development. These adults genuinely appreciate the unique beauty of the young child's artwork, whether it is a primitive representational effort, or something completely abstract. The art exhibits, musicals, and plays that result from preschoolers' efforts can be a great source of pride for children, teachers, and parents. Additionally, these times offer wonderful opportunities for parents and staff to know each other better.

He needs to be protected

Ensuring your child's safety is essential to any child care program. The young child or infant is helpless to protect himself, so caregivers must be constantly watchful. The young child needs to be protected from physical harm resulting from his own actions as well as from harm that could come from other people. Caregivers also make every effort to protect children from the spread of disease and from any food contamination.

The child enrolled in a child care program must be supervised continuously, from the time you drop him off in the morning until you pick him up in the afternoon. This includes time spent in classrooms, on the playground, while eating lunch or snacks, and throughout naptime.

Young children and infants who have begun to move around on their own will have accidents. This is part of what happens in childhood, whether at home or at school. It is not possible to protect every child from every accident, because it is the nature of young children to move quickly and impulsively. They fall and get a scratch, they bump their heads on tables and on their friends' heads, and so on. Despite this constant activity, vigilant caregivers will prevent many accidents, just as you will at home.

Obviously, when your child is enrolled in a center or family day home, she is not going to have the run of the place. She will be free to enter certain areas and find others that are closed to her. Boundaries are necessary, both indoors and out. This is for her own protection.

The Toddler Room is designed to protect the physical safety of the children in it. There are electrical outlet covers in use here, as there are in all classrooms and other areas of a child development center. There may be doorknob covers, too, so that any taller toddler with advanced fine motor skills will be unable to open the door to the playground. And the toys and equipment that children have access to in this class are designed to be safe for toddlers.

If a toddler were to enter classrooms for older children, however, there could be some problems. Children in the pre-k class use many materials and other equipment that are not safe for younger children. Often these materials contain small parts that are choking hazards for smaller preschoolers. So each classroom, from the nursery through the pre-kindergarten class, will be designed to be safe for the children it is intended for.

> EACH CLASSROOM, FROM THE NURSERY THROUGH THE PRE-KINDERGARTEN CLASS, WILL BE DESIGNED TO BE SAFE FOR THE CHILDREN IT IS INTENDED FOR.

The fire and health departments inspect centers to ensure things such as unobstructed exits and proper food storage. But while experts in these fields inspect at scheduled intervals, they don't inspect daily. So as your child's parent, you must not hesitate to ask a question of center staff, speaking up if something seems out of order in one of these areas. As you will come to understand, staff members have much to attend to, and they will appreciate your bringing to their attention anything that could be harmful to a child.

> SAFETY REQUIRES BOTH PHYSICAL AND BEHAVIORAL BOUNDARIES.

In addition to planning for safety in the design of the overall program, including its individual classrooms and playgrounds, teachers will help children learn to live within certain rules. Safety requires both physical and behavioral boundaries.

He needs discipline

Because the inappropriate use of discipline has such potentially serious consequences, I will address this topic in some greater depth.

The goal in using discipline with children, whether you are a parent or a preschool teacher, should be very positive: to help the child begin to develop self-discipline. Any adult can win in a conflict with a child, because they're bigger. But when resolving problems, a loving parent or teacher has some higher goals than merely proving her authority or having her way.

It is very important for the young child to recognize and respect the authority a supervising adult has over his life. This is vital in order to protect the child's physical safety and well-being. Instilling this attitude is easier said than done, but it is doable. To be most effective, certain fundamental understandings need to be in place, in both the mind of the adult and the child.

Efforts to force children to behave in ways they are developmentally incapable of are not productive and can be harmful. It is not reasonable to expect a two-year-old child to be able to behave like a five-year-old.

Nor can a three-year-old behave like a four-year-old. To expect such behavior of a child would be like expecting yourself to run the Boston Marathon when you sit at a desk all day and really aren't in good shape. A lot of things would have to happen before you could reasonably expect yourself to run five miles, let alone a marathon. And appropriate behavioral expectations must also be a part of any disciplinary efforts with children.

Why God Made Parents and Teachers

The reason God made parents and teachers is because children can't be left to fend for themselves. It's obvious that they need protection, provision, and guidance from us that they are unable to provide on their own or by relying on other children. Therefore, the role of the adult, whether parent or teacher, is critically important to every aspect of the child's life. This role, lovingly performed, is necessary to keep children alive and to help them develop the potentials needed for fulfilling adult lives.

In recent decades, the diversity of recommendations from the experts on how to discipline or not discipline your child has caused parents a lot of confusion. Children don't enter the world with a handbook attached to their wrist with a string. All parents who take their role seriously are vulnerable to making some mistakes while trying to do what's best. Even properly trained caregivers can make mistakes, too.

Rules Should Be Simple

Rules in the child development program should be simple and easy to understand. In our program, we had one basic rule that applied to everyone, from toddlers to five-year-olds: no hurting allowed. Children were taught that it was not okay to hurt themselves, their friends, or the things we share. They could all understand this.

Periodically, each child would be reminded of the "no hurting" rule when they crossed over this boundary or were about to do so. People were not allowed to climb up on the table because they might fall off and hurt themselves. No one was allowed to hit, throw something at, or be deliberately unkind to a friend, "because that could hurt our friend." Children weren't allowed to tear pages from a book, because then we wouldn't be able to enjoy it any longer. No hurting. This basic premise was the one from which all our rules flowed.

At times, an individual classroom of three-, four- or five-year-olds might decide they needed to make their own rule. This was often initiated by children who recognized a problem, and their teacher helped all the children involved to work this out and write it down. Most of the children could not read the rule, but they knew what it was and where it was written—an example of early self-governance. As children grew older and were promoted from class to class, they understood that the basic rules of our school remained the same. This consistency in all the classrooms, and among all the staff, was a source of confidence and security for our children.

Boundaries Are Important

Boundaries are important for all people. Our society is governed by laws. Things work best for us when everyone respects and abides by these laws. It works this way for children, too. Children thrive when they understand where the boundaries are, and the child who doesn't know where they are will keep pushing behaviorally until he finds them.

Sometimes parents seem to be confused about who is in charge and what it means to be the parent. They seem to need, above all else, for their child to like them. Perhaps the adults in their childhood were unkind or overbearing, so they've discarded the whole notion of their parental authority. They mistakenly think the freedom of living without rules will make their child happy. It is disturbing to see a grown man or woman desperately seeking the approval of their three-year-old child who regularly expresses his disapproval and disrespect by kicking Daddy in the shins or smacking Mommy in the face.

Caregivers can make the same mistake. I have visited a center where caregivers allowed children so much "freedom" that they were unable to even ensure basic safety.

Children need to know where the boundaries are, and the child who doesn't know is insecure. On some level, he understands that he is not in control and does not have the answers. He needs strong, loving adults who do know what is right and wrong for him. Their calm, confident assurance that this thing is good for him while that thing could harm him, coupled with their willingness to enforce reasonable rules, present to the child a safe place to dwell. He can be confident that he can explore his world within an established area of acceptable behavior—to try new things, fail sometimes, and try again without fear.

Capturing Children's Interest

One of the most important tools caregivers have at their disposal to avoid frustration and conflicts among children is to fill their day with a wonderful variety of interesting things to do. Appropriate planning sends the great majority of potential disciplinary problems right out the window.

Redirection

Choosing one's disciplinary battles carefully is important for not exhausting teachers and exasperating children. It is important for teachers to recognize when they should redirect children's attention away from a problem area to something new. Doing so avoids many situations that otherwise could develop into a power struggle between the adult and the child.

Redirection is especially effective for toddlers. They can be redirected easily because their attention spans are so brief. Redirection can be effective with older children as well, but it is needed less often when the child and his teacher have come to love and respect each other. Older preschoolers in this position are able to understand the reasonableness of their teacher's request and its benefit to themselves and to others.

With two-year-olds, redirection isn't always so easy. Part of the two-year-old child's work is to begin influencing and exercising some control over his environment. This is normal and healthy. The child's efforts to do this should be encouraged. However, this natural period of development can present some challenges for everyone in this young child's world. Adults are likely to hear a lot of emphatic words such as "No!" For example, imagine the teacher has announced to the class that it is outdoor playtime. When a two-year-old decides he isn't going, after the other children in the class have begun walking out, the teacher's best option may be to just pick up the child and carry him out. This may be the only way to physically protect everyone.

Consequences of Breaking Rules

It is important that there be consequences when a child crosses a boundary he or she clearly understands. Consequences help the child remember that this rule is important. If someone is unable to play with blocks without throwing them, he needs to lose his block-play privileges for a period of time. In this case, he may also need to spend some time in "time-out" to think about why we do not throw our blocks. This is a serious behavior that cannot be allowed. The intervention of the director or the child's parent may be necessary if a child persists in a potentially dangerous behavior.

Other inappropriate behaviors that don't threaten physical harm to a child can be effectively managed through understandable consequences. This often happens without a teacher's intervention, as in the case where a child says something unkind to his best friend. The friend with hurt feelings often withdraws and becomes unavailable to his little buddy, whose frustration overtook his better judgment.

Sometimes, though, the teacher must intervene and help children understand why this hard thing happened and how we can all help to set it right. Teachers often remind children that this might be a good opportunity to say "I'm sorry"—once they reach the point where facial expressions or body language tell her they actually are sorry. In some cases, when awkwardness or discomfort remains between them, the children may need another step to move past what happened. The caregiver may then ask if they would like to shake hands, or give their friend a hug. Of course, this will always be the children's decision. The ones who make this choice understand on some level that a hug or a handshake can bring closure to a troubling incident. These children often begin playing together again as if nothing had happened.

Time-Out

Time-out can be a useful tool, but to remain effective, it must not be overused. It is not appropriate for use with young toddlers. Certain children between twenty-four and thirty-six months are mature enough to understand the connection between making an inappropriate choice and needing to think about that for a moment. Three-year-olds and older are obviously capable of this understanding. Once the child has yielded to the idea that he is going to have time-out, then two minutes for a two-year-old, three minutes for a three-year-old, four minutes for a four-year-old, and so on, is usually about right. This varies somewhat from child to child. A child must never be left alone unsupervised while in time-out or at any other time. Teachers and parents should discuss and agree upon the use of this disciplinary tool.

The appropriate use of time-out is not demeaning for the child. The nature of this experience is not primarily about a reprimand or penalty. It provides an opportunity to take time to consider better ways of solving problems. Occasionally a teacher or parent may choose to take a few moments' time-out, demonstrating the value of reflecting on a problem by setting this example: "I'm taking a time-out right now. I need a minute to think about something." All children in the class come to understand the importance of setting aside a little time to reflect on a problem.

Time-out should be used only after other methods have failed to bring about the appropriate change of heart in the little offender. After the time-out period, the teacher may ask the child what he thinks about throwing blocks now. Once the child has evidenced a renewed understanding of playing in safe ways, the teacher may express her pride in his good idea and give him a reassuring hug. Often a child who has hurt another needs a hug as much as the child who has been hurt. A very young child should not have to face true sorrow and remorse over his own behavior all alone.

Spanking

Spanking—or any form of physical punishment—is entirely unacceptable in any child care center.

Patterns of Inappropriate Behavior

Sometimes a child will begin pushing against reasonable boundaries on a regular basis. If allowed to continue, the child can get himself into a pattern of inappropriate behavior. This may involve a disrespectful attitude toward teachers or friends, manifested by inappropriate language or hitting. Or it may be deliberate rule-breaking, such as coloring on other children's artwork in order to express anger or frustration. The child in this position needs some help.

In the case of a typically developing child, as opposed to one with emotional problems who obviously needs professional intervention, the key is for staff and parents to work cooperatively to break the pattern. Left to his own devices or to inappropriate adult efforts, this child can become entrenched in the behavior. When parents or teachers don't know what to do, they sometimes do more of what they've already done, with greater intensity. Adults can become frustrated and end up actually contributing to the problem with empty threats or promises or even uncontrolled anger. This works against them and the child.

Effecting Behavioral Change by Changing Our Focus
Young children always give you more of what you focus on. This is the essence of what experts in behavioral intervention implement.[2] When we want to see more kindness from our child, we must first give him kindness. If we want to see more patience, we must give him our patience. If we want our child to have more self-control, we must model self-control for him.

Even the child who has spiraled down into the distressing and, thankfully, rare circumstance that needs professional intervention eventually responds to this approach. But it cannot succeed without parental education, support, and involvement.

Every parent and caregiver can watch their preschooler's behavior very carefully and "catch the child being good."[3] Even a child who is acting out much of the time occasionally makes a good choice. When we see something we are truly proud of in this child, we need to let him know we're proud of him for that thing he did. We recognize and acknowledge his right choice, whatever it was. This must be done with a calm, honest, and genuine appreciation, because a child will recognize false praise that is really intended to manipulate him.

The child who is acting out of bounds should not be pushed away and isolated because his behavior has become difficult to handle.

This child needs to be drawn close into fellowship with teachers and parents, where he will experience the joy of the approval of his adult friends. It may take some time, but it will always work. Healthy children naturally desire the approval of loving parents and teachers.

He needs good values

We know that a large percentage of American preschoolers are spending most of their waking hours with professional caregivers. This early period in life has a significant influence on who a person becomes as an adult, including in the formation of personality, character, and values. Parents and the people who provide care for their young children need to purposefully address the important subject of teaching values. Children learn what's important about how to treat and relate with others through the example of the people who are closest to them.

Teaching good moral values in ways young children could understand was part of what we did in our center every day. We recognized that leading children to appreciate these values in their lives at day care needed to be an extension of what parents were teaching them at home. Otherwise, children would be receiving mixed messages from home and school about some really important life issues. For this reason, we were careful to address this subject with all parents who were considering enrolling in our program. They and we needed to be assured that we agreed on certain fundamentals, to protect children from the confusion that would otherwise result.

Despite the diverse cultures and religions of our families, I don't remember any parent expressing concern about this portion of our developmental curriculum. To the contrary, they enthusiastically supported us in this effort.

Discussions related to this part of everyday life took place between caregivers and the individual children who were ready to begin thinking about how our behavior affects others and how we treat our friends. This was not done in an especially structured way but simply as a matter of course in our center's daily life. Natural opportunities arose to talk about these things, and our teachers would engage one or two children about good ways of relating with others. Through such moments and through the caregiver's personal example, children began to appreciate values such as:

🌱 FRIENDSHIP—by acknowledging that our friends, both children and adults, are important to us. We enjoy playing and learning together. We care about our friends, and they care about us. Our days are more interesting and fun because we have friends, and we miss them when they are not with us.

🌱 KINDNESS—by helping children remember that we feel better when our friends are kind to us. They feel happy, too, when we remember to be kind.

> CHILDREN LEARN THROUGH THE EXAMPLE OF THE PEOPLE WHO ARE CLOSEST TO THEM.

🌱 SELF-CONTROL—by supporting children appropriately when they lose control, reminding them of a variety of good ways to express frustration or anger. Hitting is not allowed because hitting hurts. But it's okay to draw a really mad picture or to talk about how very, very mad we are. As the song goes, "When you're angry and you know it, stomp your feet."[4]

🌱 SHARING—by reminding the child to notice his friend's happy face when he shares the special library book or allows his friend a turn at the computer. Over time, young children can catch a glimpse of the joy of sharing when they begin to grow beyond their natural self-interest to recognize and also care about the interests and needs of others.

🌱 GENEROSITY—by helping a preschooler make a special gift to take home, such as painting a smooth stone with bright colors to be used as a paperweight. Children recognize the blessings they receive as they observe their parents' delight at the surprise.

- PATIENCE—by learning to take turns at the water fountain or waiting to speak while a classmate shares something important. Young children can begin the process of developing some capacity to be content during times of waiting.
- HONESTY—by avoiding scolding or harsh criticism of a child who acknowledges that he's done something wrong or made a mistake, caregivers create an environment of freedom to tell the truth.
- GRATITUDE—by offering a prayer of thanksgiving at mealtime, to thank the Giver of the food. Not all people have the blessings we often take for granted, and it is important for all of us, including our young children, to live in such bounty with a spirit of thankfulness. Children more readily learn gratitude when they are taught to say "Thank you" to the people around them and to the Giver of every good and perfect gift.
- RESPECT FOR OTHERS—by not pushing and shoving on the way out to the playground. Using good manners is orderly and respectful and avoids hurting others and ourselves. Children need to learn that all people are important and deserve to be treated honorably. By this action, we say to those around us, "You are important, too, and I care about that. I will show you that you matter to me by the way I treat you, even when I'm really in a hurry to get outside to play."

These values were presented and discussed so children could understand that treating people well need not be burdensome. Rather, when we invest our time and our hearts to treat them the way we would like to be treated, good things naturally come to us, too. Children discovered for themselves that caring about others brings joy to us, as we learn to take pleasure in the good things this value brings to them. In time, our thoughtful treatment of others will have a positive effect on how they treat us. The wisdom of the Golden Rule remains true for us today: "...whatever you wish that others would do to you, do also to them..."[5]

5

STARTING YOUR SEARCH

hen Zack's parents were making financial plans before he was born, including the decision to enroll their son in day care at the age of two, they weren't overly concerned about this part of the arrangement. Since day care was available everywhere and all the young couples they knew used these services, they took for granted that everything would work out fine for Zack. They didn't anticipate the need to inform themselves about this decision, looking at it instead as if it were nothing more momentous than finding a clean, convenient family restaurant.

Their perspective on this subject did not reflect the value they placed on their child. They loved Zack and wanted the very best for him. They just hadn't thought through what this significant change in their lifestyle would mean to their child and to themselves. Nor had they considered the important reasons for their little boy's love for play and what was really happening in his life as he engaged in play at home with Mom or when visiting friends. They were not aware that the details of how any child development program functions would make such a big difference in the moment to moment and hour to hour of little Zack's daily life. The result was that they and their child suffered some needless distress. Given their circumstances, it was an easy mistake to make.

THE INVESTMENT OF TIME IT TAKES PARENTS TO EDUCATE themselves about child care will pay big dividends in their family's life.

REFERRAL RESOURCES

Regulatory departments and referral agencies

A relatively small percentage of the workforce is fortunate to have child care provided on-site by their employer. If you are one of the fortunate few and space is available when you need care, this may be your answer. Or your employer might have a referral program to help employees find child care. This may work well for you, and you may find the right program right away. Usually, however, a family is on its own. They must start at the beginning.

Numerous practical resources are available to parents beginning a search for child care services. Many governmental regulatory departments or child care resource and referral agencies will give you factual information such as licensing status, which centers are most conveniently located, what ages of children they serve, whether they provide transportation, hours of operation, and so on. This is a very important part of what you need to know, but it will not likely address some of your deeper concerns for your child. It's not always easy to determine whether the person or agency from whom you're gathering information shares your priorities on behalf of young children.

Family, friends, and associates

Starting with your family members and friends, or with business or professional associates, is one of the best places to begin searching, because you know these people and understand some things about what matters to them. Getting a good reference from someone you know and respect, such as from a coworker or family physician, who has used a particular child care program and feels great about it, could be a huge benefit to you. An individual whose value system is close to yours is a great source of security as you look for a placement for your child; however, no person's recommendation can ever be a substitute for your own considered judgment. If this is someone you're close to, and their child is still enrolled, the connection may afford the opportunity of a casual visit to your friend's program one afternoon at pick-up time or at morning drop-off. If you keep your eyes and ears open, you'll gather lots of valuable information about the center in such a visit.

> NO PERSON'S RECOMMENDATION CAN EVER BE A SUBSTITUTE FOR YOUR OWN CONSIDERED JUDGMENT.

CHURCHES AND OTHER RELIGIOUS ORGANIZATIONS

If you've just moved to town and don't really know anybody, a call to a local church or other community religious organization could be very helpful. Many pastors or members of their church staff are happy to set aside some time to visit with a newcomer to the community. Of course, they'd love for you and your family to attend their church, but that's not their only motive. These people's life work is about serving others, and they'll understand how concerned you are about the right placement in day care for your child. Many churches and synagogues provide child care services through good programs that are open to community enrollment. Additionally, church secretaries may know fellow members who offer good family day home arrangements, with regulatory oversight, for small groups of children. Or they may know of someone who offers infant or toddler care for two or three little ones and may be able to ask a friend who has used this service to contact you with a reference.

Grade school teachers

You may be able to gain valuable insights into a particular child development program by asking a kindergarten teacher. A friend or acquaintance may have a friend who teaches in the grade school your child will be attending. These are the people who have the first opportunity to know individual preschoolers coming into grade school. If they have been pleased with the readiness of children, including their pre-academic readiness and their social and emotional maturity, who have come from a particular center, they may be willing to share their confidence in that program. Sometimes these teachers' own children will have been enrolled there. Grade school principals are often aware of such programs as well.

> IF YOU'RE NEW TO TOWN, A CALL TO A LOCAL CHURCH COULD BE VERY HELPFUL.

The internet

Many child care centers have their own Web sites. They may include practical information such as hours of operation, ages of children served, a map to their location, and so on. The site may also include information about the program's curriculum, their philosophy regarding their work, and opportunities for parents to become involved. There may even be some photographs of their center, which will help give you a feel for what this program is like before you visit.

Although a Web site can provide insight into a particular program, do not rule out a program just because it isn't online. Many of the best programs were established years ago and have such a solid reputation that having a Web site would actually generate more tours than they could manage.

On the other hand, just because a center has an appealing Web site doesn't necessarily mean it will provide the quality your child needs. Use the Internet to help identify potential programs but never use it as a shortcut for selecting one.

The Director of the Program You Can't Get Into

If your top-choice center is unable to accommodate your child, ask the director or his staff if there is another program in their area known for its quality. Ask where they would go and why, if they were in your position.

The Yellow Pages™

Don't forget the value of looking in the phone book's advertising section. In addition to some practical info in each center's ad, such as a map, you can often get a sense of a program's perspective on their work and the children they serve. The aesthetic choices in their advertisement and, indeed, the very name of their organization, may say a lot about them.

Some centers have names that reduce the concept of child care to something grossly simplistic. Others include tasteless caricatures of children in their advertisements. Things like this may simply indicate a very limited aesthetic sense on the part of the program's owner or a poor choice of names—there probably are perfectly wonderful places for children with ads or names that you or I would not have chosen. On the other hand, the name choice may reflect an inadequate appraisal of who children really are and what work with them should be all about.

Taken alone, observations like these are not adequate to judge the center's merits. However, a program with a thoughtless name or an

> USE THE INTERNET TO IDENTIFY POTENTIAL PROGRAMS, BUT NEVER AS A SHORTCUT FOR SELECTING ONE.

ad whose design makes light of children has a credibility deficit that would have to be made up to me before I could seriously consider those folks as care providers for my child.

GATHERING BASIC INFORMATION

Making the call

Let's assume you've begun talking with some folks about your need for care and have a list of potential centers. You've decided to start first with programs that seem to provide quality, are within your price range, and will be convenient to work or home. You know they enroll children of your child's age. Now you need to start making calls.

Confirm with the director or staff of each program the information you've gathered from others. For example, the fact that a center once provided care for infants does not guarantee they still do, or their hours of operation may have shifted somewhat. Child care is labor-intensive, and as costs rise, sometimes difficult choices must be made. So go ahead and assure yourself that your starting information is up-to-date.

Prepare a list of questions you want to ask each director when you call. Also, take notes about each program during the conversation (or immediately afterward), so you can keep it all straight in the midst of what is, for most of us, a very emotional time.

Is space available? What about a waiting list?

At some point in the conversation, you'll want to find out whether this program has room for your child. However, I recommend you avoid asking this question too soon. The search for quality child care takes time, and you will want to streamline your efforts as you become accustomed to the search process. In the beginning, though, you'll learn a great deal just by listening to directors or their assistants when you call for general information about their program.

If the person you're speaking to immediately says they don't have any space available, you can still say, "I'm just starting to look, and I'm feeling a little overwhelmed. Could you please take a moment to give me some ideas about what I should be looking for?" Or "Maybe you know of another program close to you that is known to have high quality..."

It's always possible the person you're speaking with may be unable to spend any more time on the phone. But if he or she does have a few minutes, most who are involved in this work for the right reasons will be willing to offer some direction to a caller. They will care about what you're going through. If she is curt and dismissive, this probably isn't a place you'd want for your child anyway.

WAITING LISTS CAN BE TRICKY.

As you converse with this person, you'll begin to have a sense of whether this is a program that meets your basic criteria and merits a closer look. Then you can ask whether the program has available space. The best programs often have long waiting lists. Sometimes the list will require a fee to place your name on it. Ask for the director's best estimate of the next available open space for your child.

Even if you're told there will be no space for your child until next year, don't give up! If you think this might be a place you'd love, consider touring the center—despite the apparent obstacle of the waiting list. If a tour confirms a parent's interest, some will consider getting on the list anyway with a plan to transfer when space opens.

Many mothers place their unborn infant or older preschooler on the lists of several programs, despite the likely nonrefundable fee just to be on the list of each one. This is a way families protect themselves, increasing the chance that at least one program they prefer will actually have a spot when they need it. But waiting lists can be tricky. Sometimes an expected space will not open up because an infant scheduled to advance at twelve months does not yet have the developmental readiness for all the activity of the Toddler Room. In other cases, three or four centers expecting the same child to enroll in their program within a particular time frame learn that child is enrolling elsewhere. When that family informs those directors they've decided to enroll somewhere else, one of them may have an unexpected opening that no one else on their waiting list is prepared to take. That space may be available to you. The point is, don't give up! Miracles do happen.

Ask one more question

It is always possible that the program you prefer has a long, active waiting list, and the director is unable even to offer you a tour. If so, before you hang up, take time to ask her one more question: "What do you think is the most important thing your program offers for children?" If she has a few minutes to talk further, what comes next could give you real insight into how a good director thinks about her work. You may learn her perspective on the young child, what her goals are in providing child care services, and how she feels about her staff and the parent group she serves.

Most good directors are passionate about their work and—given the time—are glad to share what they think is really important in an environment for young children. You might be surprised at the insights gained through such a conversation—insights into this particular program, and what's important in other good programs in your community.

QUALITY CLUES OVER THE PHONE

Be prepared—getting through may take time

The timing of your call may be such that neither the director nor her assistants are available to talk with you. One may be giving a parent tour while the other is in a staff meeting. Or one may be at the school supply store while the other is at the grocery because the milk delivery accidentally shorted her by two gallons. Or a teacher may be ill and someone from the office staff is needed in the classroom to fill in for her until her substitute arrives. Or the director may be attempting to support an upset parent concerned about his or her absent spouse's inattention to their child, while the health department has stopped in to see whether there's adequate soap in the dispensers of all the restrooms. And if that's not enough, Toddler II's toilet has stopped up because someone wanted to see if his rubber ducky would go down and the teacher can't get the valve to shut off. Well, you get the picture!

Having the kind of staff some university, hospital, or even church centers can afford is a distant dream for most directors. If the director isn't available, you may want to leave your name and number or try again later. The phones in our center were ringing much of the time. And while the assistant director and our administrative assistant were usually in their offices to answer the phones, sometimes all of us were otherwise engaged. If you think this program is a good one, then persist.

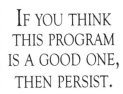

IF YOU THINK THIS PROGRAM IS A GOOD ONE, THEN PERSIST.

Listen for quality clues

When you do reach someone, listen for clues to quality. Some of the most important clues deal with how the staff treats others. If you've heard great things about a program you call and you happen to get someone who seems rushed or short, you may want to give her the benefit of the doubt, and avoid taking offense. Consider that there may be a reasonable explanation and try later. But when you try again, you should expect that even though you're not part of their program yet, you will be treated with courtesy and respect. There should be a tone of caring and helpfulness toward you and your needs. An attitude of joyful service should pervade this building.

Background sounds

Another opportunity to learn about a program's quality is to listen to what you hear in the background. You might hear two staff members talking together in a tone that speaks of their mutual respect for each other and their enthusiasm for their work. Or the phone might be answered by a classroom teacher expecting a call back from one of her parents. If you hear tension and chaos every time you call a center, you should be very concerned. On the other hand, you may hear lots of little voices talking at once. They should sound engaged and happy, excited or relaxed . . . at home.

SCHEDULE A TOUR

Touring a center at various times of the day provides particular benefits, and, naturally, there will be important things to observe throughout the day. If after your initial tour you can return for the whole day, that is ideal and you should do so. Of course, not all parents can spend that much time. You should, however, schedule some amount of extended observation time with the director of a center on your short list.

Whether you are there for an extended visit or for a shorter one, don't expect to be free to wander around the campus unescorted the way enrolled parents do. But a director who is proud of her program will be glad for you to spend some extra time in your child's prospective classroom, possibly even joining the children and staff for lunch. A good program's policies will have restrictions on touring for the sake of security and minimizing disruptions to the classroom environments. You may want to tour several times and at various times of the day.

In Part Four, "The Tour," we walk through a high-quality child development program together so you will be equipped to evaluate what you observe when you tour the centers you are considering. The remainder of this chapter has brief descriptions of what to expect if you tour at midmorning, lunchtime, or midafternoon, so you can consider what you'll see during visits at various times of the day. You'll then be able to select a time for your tour that you feel is most advantageous for you.

Prepare to focus on what you see

If at all possible, don't bring your child at first. To make a wise decision, your focus needs to be entirely on the program, not on your child's response to it. That will come later.

The midmorning tour

When you tour midmorning, you'll have the opportunity to see the children engaged in all kinds of interesting activities: some child-directed, some teacher-directed. As you move from one classroom to another, you will notice that the number and length of teacher-directed activities increases with older groups. Story time in the toddler class is often quite brief. There will usually be a couple of little guys who just don't want a story right then. They sit with their teacher and friends for only a moment or two and then are up and off again. They're interested in other things, and that's just fine.

On the other hand, group time in pre-k is more like what occurs in a kindergarten class. The children's capacity to remain engaged has grown, and most understand—others are learning—that we take turns talking at group time. As a friend gets to speak and other children hold on to their ideas, they grow in patience, self-control, and generosity. In another year, these children will be in kindergarten—even more mature and ready for the longer periods of whole-class involvement that will be part of that experience.

An appropriate developmental curriculum encompasses every aspect and time frame of the child's day, but the midmorning tour allows you to observe its structure and function in ways that may be easier to recognize. After all, in the morning, everyone is rested and ready for new experiences. For example, you may see children in circle time discussing their topic of study for the week, which could range from airports to zebras.

When circle time is over, children move to activity centers that are set up to provide experiences that, in a variety of ways, support learning more about the topic of the week. But the topic of the week is actually just a springboard for the more significant kinds of learning taking place. Children learn as they interact with other children and as they access a wide variety of interesting equipment and materials that foster their growth.

The preschooler's learning style is different from that of a teenager in high school, who acquires most information in lecture, research, or discussion formats. Much of the young child's manner of learning involves getting their hands on things. To many adults, this looks like they are "just playing." Watching closely will help you understand the breadth of learning taking place, suited to each child's developmental level.

The Lunchtime Tour
Lunchtime in the Nursery

At lunchtime, expect things to be really busy. In a well-managed nursery, staff members anticipate the babies' needs before they occur. It's actually possible for a caregiver to feed three or four infants within an acceptable time frame, without too much fuss. I'm speaking here of experienced caregivers, of course. Each baby is satisfied because he is fed when hungry and his meal is not rushed.

As you are aware, feeding just one baby when you're a new parent can be overwhelming at first. In a good center, simple systems are in place that facilitate feeding several infants, since the entire orientation of the caregivers is meeting babies' needs. While lunchtime is one of the most demanding times of the day for caregivers, our parents were always amazed. Frankly, I was, too.

Lunchtime with Toddlers and Preschoolers

After everyone's hands are washed—itself a very interesting process to observe—older children, from toddlers to preschoolers, are seated at the table with their friends and teachers. Everyone looks forward to this time. And there will be a lot more going on than just eating the food and drinking the milk.

It takes patience and skill for a preschool teacher to direct a group of two-year-olds, or four- and five-year-olds for that matter, into the ideal mealtime experience. Some days this works better than others, but it will always be her goal that this be a pleasant, relaxed period. The teacher is actively engaged with her children. Children converse with her and their friends, very much as they would at home with their families. You may hear children discussing what they liked best about their morning activities or the new puppy or the new baby who just moved into their house.

> AT FIRST, YOUR FOCUS NEEDS TO BE ENTIRELY ON THE PROGRAM, NOT ON YOUR CHILD'S RESPONSE TO IT.

You can see here the opportunities for learning in the areas of language and social and emotional development. It is a privilege to watch a child move beyond only what's important to her and begin to take pleasure in listening to what's important to someone else.

Your tour may take place on a day when one of the children's parents has joined the group for lunch, and this affords another dimension to what you observe. In the best programs, community is formed among children, staff, and parents. And you will note that this parent knows and is comfortable with all the children, and they know and like him or her, too.

The midafternoon tour

Afternoon tours provide the opportunity to see how things are as children and staff begin to get a little tired. The staff may start to sag, but their professionalism should not. Our program, like many others, had a supplemental staff of full-time college students who worked part-time for us. They arrived in our classrooms each afternoon between 12:30 and 3:00 and worked until closing. In certain rooms, they helped with lunch-to-naptime transitions and covered all full-time caregivers' breaks during naps. Those who worked between 3:00 and 6:00 provided staffing transition for the children as well as other support for full-time, opening staff who left between 4:00 and 4:30.

Our part-time staff's presence was beneficial for several reasons. As teachers began to slow down a little as the day progressed, an extra staff member shared between one or two full-time teachers had obvious practical value. Also, their arrival into the program each day was like a breath of fresh air, since they were often eager to know all about the children's day and were excited to see their little friends. They seemed to have no end to their own energy reserves. The fact that afternoon staff would arrive soon also gave an emotional lift to the full-time staff who were beginning to need this relief.

> OUR PROGRAM, LIKE MANY OTHERS, HAD A SUPPLEMENTAL STAFF OF COLLEGE STUDENTS WHO WORKED PART-TIME.

When naptime is over, children typically spend time in activity centers and on the playground. The scheduled order of things is a little different from what is found during tours scheduled earlier in the day. But you will still see children engaged with their teachers and with each other, just at a somewhat more relaxed and less-structured pace.

PART THREE

Inside the Business of Child Care

6

CENTER POLICIES

asey Timms was a single mother with a fourteen-month-old daughter named Darla. Unlike most of the single mothers I had met, Casey seemed pretty carefree. Darla adjusted readily to the toddler class, and Casey was pleased.

Casey's manner of relating to the staff was always very friendly and chatty, but maybe just a little too familiar. The caregivers frequently heard all about Casey's plans for the evening, which often didn't include her child. She repeatedly asked caregivers to sit with Darla in her home, without getting prior approval from our director. Doing so would have been against our staff policies, which protected against caregivers becoming too tired from nighttime work with young children to be able to provide what our children needed during the day. But, then, Casey didn't seem concerned about any of our policies.

In the first several months, she always had an excuse for why her tuition check needed to be held rather than deposited. After several of Casey's checks were late or returned, I informed her that this problem must not occur again or she would have to make other arrangements. The following month, her child's tuition was paid by Casey's mother.

From that time on, the grandmother called me periodically to see if everything was all right with Darla. Although Grandmother seemed somewhat anxious, everything was fine with Darla. She was happy at school, exploring her classroom, playing alongside the other toddlers, and enjoying her caregivers. She was a delightful child. We didn't observe anything that would have raised a red flag.

Soon after the tuition payment problem had been satisfactorily resolved, Casey began arriving later and later each afternoon at pick-up time. First, she was just a minute or two late, then five minutes, then twenty. We asked parents to be present no later than 5:55 p.m., to accommodate our closing time at 6:00. (Most of our late-afternoon staffers were college students, and some of them had to be back to their campus by 6:30 to avoid missing dinner. We had learned long before that we would lose staff members who were imposed on by parents who disregarded the staff's need to attend to their own families or other personal responsibilities.)

The first time I addressed the late pick-up problem with Casey, she apologized and assured me it wouldn't happen again. But it did, within a matter of days. This time, Casey didn't arrive at all. Instead, she sent her new boyfriend. He had been drinking.

Since Casey was unavailable at any of her contact numbers, we called Darla's grandmother to inform her of this predicament. Of course, she was alarmed and came immediately to pick up the toddler. After all was said and done, we all left the center that evening around 7:00 p.m. Needless to say, this family had to make other arrangements for their little girl, since their special needs were beyond our capacity.

WHAT A POLICY STATEMENT REVEALS

A good way to gain insight into the mechanics of how a center functions is through the lens of its policies. The parent policy statement will inform you of what the center needs from you in order to provide the services you need for your child. Whether you choose a family day home or a larger child care center, all parents and staff need to agree on certain issues that affect the children. Understanding some of these will sharpen your observation skills when you actually tour the centers you are considering. If the center you're most interested in is not required by law to provide a policy statement, consider using the information in this chapter to help formulate your list of questions for the director.

When you enroll your child into a program of quality, you may question why certain of its policies even need to be addressed. But it is safe to assume that the people who established the policies have seen some contingencies you might not expect and that each of the policies was instituted for the well-being of everyone involved.

Reading a strong policy statement is reassuring for parents, because it indicates the responsible parties have thought deeply about this work and have taken time to structure the parent/center relationship to protect and benefit everyone. This section will give examples of some of the issues an effective policy statement will address and explain some of the rationale behind the rules. Why are there so many rules? In a nutshell, the answer to that question is day care is complicated.

> A STRONG POLICY STATEMENT ASSURES YOU RESPONSIBLE PARTIES HAVE THOUGHT DEEPLY ABOUT THIS WORK.

CHILD CARE CENTERS AND THEME PARKS

In certain ways, a good center works like a theme park. If you have ever visited Disney World, you probably experienced what my family and I experienced there—it's just fun. Fun rides, shows, and architecture. Pretty gardens. Staff members who make you feel welcome.

There's easy access to fast food so you can stay all day and not think about cooking. Music is selected and piped into areas crowded with long lines. All these elements and more combine to help you just relax and enjoy this great place with your friends and family.

Once you get back home, it may occur to you, as it did to me, that it takes a lot of "behind-the-scenes" work to accomplish that welcoming, relaxing, fun atmosphere. In fact, there's a whole underground system of tunnels, storage rooms, dressing rooms, security control areas, and so on, running beneath the entire complex. Lots of people are there working very hard to create what we experience as fun.

> YOU AND YOUR CHILD SHOULD BE ABLE TO RELAX AND ENJOY YOUR CENTER AS YOU COME AND GO EACH DAY.

You and your child should be able to relax and enjoy your center as you come and go each day, without worrying about the complex mechanics that facilitate its pleasing atmosphere.

CHILD CARE CENTERS AND HOSPITALS

A child care center's administration also has some similarities to hospital administration. A hospital's services are directed toward patients with highly individualized needs. Even when two patients have exactly the same illness with the same treatment protocol, each of them will respond to treatment in his or her individual way. Hospital staff must be quick to alter therapies as the individual patient's needs dictate.

Patients experiencing illness and infirmity are vulnerable. Their time in the hospital and the quality of its staff can dramatically affect their future health. So it is for children in day care. They, too, are vulnerable. Their time in child care and the quality of center staff can affect their future dramatically.

The individuality of children's physical, emotional, social, cognitive, and spiritual needs must be anticipated and planned for. And staff must be knowledgeable about meeting all these needs. They must be quick to respond compassionately and alter course when something's not working right for an individual child.

IT'S NOT CHILD'S PLAY

Child care is not child's play. Many individuals and groups, including thoughtful, well-motivated, and well-funded groups, have failed at attempting this endeavor. I believe this is because they simply never appreciated, or they misunderstood, what it takes to do it right. Child care is serious business. Parents who enrolled into our program were required to sign a statement saying they agreed to abide by our program's policies while their child remained enrolled.

> CONSIDER WHETHER THIS PROGRAM IS OPERATED THOUGHTFULLY ENOUGH TO EARN YOUR TRUST.

WHAT A STRONG POLICY STATEMENT MAY LOOK LIKE

An effective statement of parent policies will address many concerns, just as each center's policies for staff members will cover a wide range of issues particular to them. The following categories of concerns are the ones our center's parent policies addressed; other programs may have additional categories to suit their unique organizational demands. Each of the remaining subsections of this chapter is intended to identify those categories and reveal some of the reasons why these policies are important—not provide specific language you should look for. My goal here is to get you thinking along these lines so you will be equipped to consider whether a prospective program is operated thoughtfully enough to earn your trust.

The Nature of the Organization

The center will designate whether it is for-profit or not-for-profit as well as any religious affiliation it may have. It will define ages of children served and something about the nature of the child development program's goals. There may be a statement of admissions policy regarding race, religion, and national origin. And a reference to admission of children with handicapping conditions may be included.

Hours of Operation

The policy statement will inform you of the program's typical hours of operation each week. Any exceptions during the year for holidays or teacher in-service days will be referenced.

Policies regarding inclement weather will be delineated. Centers may use the services of local television and radio stations to announce to the community when treacherous weather conditions will require their program's early closing. They may also provide an information hotline so parents can call in for the latest news regarding an early closing or late opening, due to snow or ice.

Paperwork Parents Provide

Expect a good program to require you to complete all paperwork related to your child's enrollment prior to the first day of school. In addition to this initial paperwork, parents are responsible for keeping all required information updated. Failure to provide your center with current information could jeopardize your child's position in the program. Such a failure could put other families at risk as well. In addition to maintaining many other standards of practice, the status of a program's license depends upon careful compliance with regulatory law that requires current information.

Agents of the health department and those of the state agency that oversees child care centers periodically stop by unannounced to examine children's records. The staff's time is best spent improving the quality of the day for all children enrolled. If a parent fails to provide the necessary paperwork, thereby creating a threat to the program's licensing status, then busy staff members spend valuable time tracking down one or more critical types of information.

Emergency Medical Authorization

Part of what you will need to agree to is the center's right to procure emergency medical care for your child in the unlikely event it should be needed. Having this documentation on-site in your child's file is obviously important, because sometimes parents are not immediately available.

What if you were to become ill suddenly while at work? Your and your coworkers' focus would be on taking care of you. If your illness were the result of, say, food poisoning from a meal at home, your child might be affected the same way. You might not be available to send faxes back and forth. Without your signature for medical care authorization, center staff would have no right to obtain medical care for your child. And hospital staff would have no legal authority to treat your child, possibly complicating and delaying their efforts at what could be a critical time.

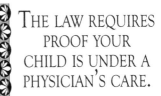

THE LAW REQUIRES PROOF YOUR CHILD IS UNDER A PHYSICIAN'S CARE.

Health Record

Another ongoing need of licensed centers is a current health record from your child's pediatrician. Centers are required by law to keep these records to prove that each child enrolled is under the care of a physician. In addition to a health history, this record contains the doctor's signature affirming your child is current with immunizations and free of communicable illness. Parents are responsible for keeping the center supplied with a current health record.

Current Contact Information

Centers must know how to contact children's parents quickly. They will require you to provide your employer's name, address, and phone number. They also need to know your home address and your cell and home phone numbers.

In addition, your center will need the name of a person you authorize to act for you on behalf of your child in any emergency. While we don't expect an emergency situation to occur, it is imperative that we think about what could possibly happen with young children and plan for any such eventuality.

It really is not sufficient to just supply your center with the name of an emergency contact person, check this requirement off your list, and forget about it. Parents must periodically confirm that this individual understands the importance of his or her availability and make certain all contact information is current. Parents must be diligent about reporting in writing any changes in their or their emergency contact person's information.

EMERGENCY PROCEDURES

Parents are informed of what would happen in the event of an emergency. You need to know your center's planned procedures in case of severe illness or injury. You should also be informed about plans for children if for any reason the building had to be evacuated—for example, our center had a "sister center" relationship with another program two blocks away. Were I starting a program today, I would give careful thought to common-sense measures needed in the event of a neighborhood- or city-wide evacuation caused by an industrial accident, natural disaster, or terrorist attack.

Arrival/departure procedures

Arrival and departure of children must be orderly and systematic. A good program will provide a place where everyone develops the sense of being at their "home away from home." However, parents must never feel so much at home that they become casual about dropping their child off at school. Afternoon departure must also be carefully controlled. Some centers help ensure security of their building through a keypad entry. All good programs employ methods ensuring children's safety and security throughout each day.

Morning Drop-off

Most programs cannot afford to have a staff member designated to receive children at the door in the mornings. In a typical program, children arrive any time between seven and nine o'clock, so centers require parents to come into the classroom with their child each morning. The parent or the teacher will sign the child in for the day. Some programs use computers for the daily sign-in/sign-out function, while others use paper records.

It is never acceptable to let an older preschooler exit an automobile alone, allowing the child to enter the building while parents watch from the car. These brief minutes saved for drive time could place the child at grave risk. Just when you think you know the parameters of a given child's behavior, they'll surprise you. This is because of ongoing development in these early years. A child who is given freedom to walk to class alone might decide to turn and walk right back out for an extra good-bye hug after the parent drives away.

Children and staff need parents to enter the child's classroom every morning at greeting time for another reason. Doing so sends important messages to the child about the parent's involvement in his or her life at school and of the child's teacher as a person important to the family.

Afternoon Pick-up

Center policies likewise address afternoon departures. Parents inform the staff, in writing, precisely who is allowed to pick up their child. Parents should expect this documentation to be kept in the child's file. This list may change periodically, and any changes in a parent's approved pick-up list should promptly be given to the director in writing.

Typically, parents or an authorized aunt or uncle or friend will sign the child out for the day. Unfortunately, there are times when a judge must rule against a natural parent picking up or visiting his or her own child. In our state, we had no legal right to prevent this without a copy of this official ruling from the custodial parent. With that document in our possession, we were justified in calling the police if the noncustodial parent arrived on center property.

Upholding your caregiver's rules

Once parents enter their child's presence at pick-up time, the child's perception of who is in authority over him—parent or teacher—naturally changes. A child may begin testing for himself who is in charge. Sometimes children's behavior patterns change dramatically when adults have not anticipated this problem and the child observes the adults' resulting uncertainty. He may deliberately violate important safety rules in the presence of his teacher and parent to see what will happen. Potentially dangerous behaviors can develop unless the center and parents decide ahead of time that teachers continue to have authority over the child while he or she is still in the building or on the playground. This avoids confusion and reinforces healthy concepts of authority.

Parental support of a teacher's rules must be unequivocal for the protection of all children in the group. This sends the message of a united front on the part of all adults and elicits cooperation from children in the important area of safety rules.

> PARENTAL SUPPORT OF CAREGIVERS' RULES MUST BE UNEQUIVOCAL, TO PROTECT ALL CHILDREN.

Impaired drivers

No center should ever release a child to a parent or authorized pick-up person who stopped by a bar after work and arrives at the center impaired. Centers should happily risk offending a parent before releasing his or her child to an impaired driver, even if the driver happens to be the child's parent. The police department can help with any such situation. And it's good to address this issue in the policy statement, while cool heads are prevailing.

Tuition and fees

You should be informed of tuition payment policies. Some programs allow parents to pay weekly, while others require a monthly payment in advance. The consequences of late payment or nonpayment of tuition should be addressed.

As costs rise, centers must increase tuition. This should be done in an orderly manner, allowing parents as much notice as possible. Your center may announce annually any projected percentage increase and when it will take effect.

Typically, centers have other fees in addition to tuition. These fees often include annual registration and supply fees. The policy statement should define the amounts and how each fee is spent. Extracurricular class fees should be explained as well as any transportation or field-trip fees. If there is a fee for late payment or for late pick-up of your child, you should be informed here, too.

Most centers require full tuition payment, even when a child is out sick or when families take vacation or take the day off together on holidays. Stable programs usually do not provide drop-in child care services, so they have no way to make up any funding deficit that would occur if they did not charge for predictable or unpredictable absences. Staff salaries and mortgage or lease payments continue whether or not an individual child is present. The critical benefit to you is that your center continues holding your child's spot while he or she is absent for any reason, turning away other families who need care.

Insurance

The policy statement will include information on whether or not this program provides health insurance for its enrolled children. Most do not and may ask you to provide proof that you have health insurance to cover your child in the event of an accident while in the center's care.

Trial enrollment

Every child is unique, and not every child will do well in a large child care program. Some are more comfortable in a smaller family day home. Parents and teachers aren't always able to know whether this is the right placement or not, unless the child is actually enrolled.

Some programs provide for a routine trial enrollment period for the child who has never been in day care before. During this period, as for all children, every effort will be made to help the child in his or her adjustment to preschool. Over time, however, if it's obviously not working, the program may give reasonable notice to parents so they can make another arrangement that better suits the child's needs.

Withdrawal

Expect your center to protect its program by requiring a thirty-day notice of withdrawal from the program. There are good reasons for this requirement. Most days of the week, good programs receive inquiries about enrollment. Some of these calls are from people who lose interest upon hearing the price of tuition. But many parents are interested and would enroll if an opening were occurring soon.

When parents leave without adequate notice, they take from the center a critical component it needs to function properly—consistent funding. When centers have proper notice that a child is leaving, they have time to replace that child with another child of like age, thus keeping their program full. Inadequate notice not only strains the finances, but it also adds administrative burdens and undermines the stability the other families rely on. Whether your program is for profit or nonprofit, the small percentage of total enrollment that makes it all work would probably surprise you.

Everyone who needs to make a change has a special reason. But parents must recognize the importance of their commitment to give notice and how failure to do this affects everyone else. A quality program will rightfully expect you to abide by all policies, including this one.

Center policy changes

From time to time a center may need to add a new policy, or alter an existing one. The policy statement may include an explanation of how changes to center policies are implemented. Some programs may allow parents a defined period of time for objecting to such changes.

In our program, arrangements were available at our option to either allow parents to withdraw their child without the typical notice or be exempted from a given policy change during the required withdrawal notice period.

Notices to parents

Expect your caregivers and management staff to keep you informed about matters affecting your child, his class, or the center as a whole. Notices will typically be posted at one or more places convenient for your review during pick-up or drop-off time. Some centers will put a duplicate copy in your child's cubby. It is the responsibility of parents to read and respond accordingly to the center's notices about important issues affecting your child.

Parent/staff communications

From infancy through pre-kindergarten, expect some daily written communication from your child's primary caregiver. You need to know certain information about your child's day, every day. The nature of this information changes as children grow older, but the need for basic communication between center staff and the child's parent does not. This daily report should be only the foundation of information exchange. Other opportunities for sharing information about your child will occur as you come and go each day and have time to visit with your child's caregivers.

> EXPECT SOME WRITTEN COMMUNICATION FROM YOUR CHILD'S PRIMARY CAREGIVER EVERY DAY.

Expect to receive a special accident report if your child is injured. You need to know how, why, and when this happened, as well as any first aid given by the caregiver. Even when an injury was minor, like a small scratch, our staff always called a child's parent right away.

An incident report informs you of circumstances involving more than one child—if your child hurt or was hurt by another child. The report will not include the name of the other child but will describe what happened and when, and how it was resolved.

Absences

Parents will be asked to notify the center when their child will be absent. Staff members should not have to wonder whether the child might be sick with a communicable illness. If your child is ill, the staff needs to be watchful of symptoms in other children, for the protection of all.

Center caregivers will appreciate the courtesy of your informing them if you're just staying home with your child for the day, too. This way they have an answer for your child's friends, who may be asking where she is.

Illness

Children showing signs of communicable illness must not be brought into the center, placing other children at risk. When a child becomes ill during the day, centers will expect parents to pick up their child at once. The sick child will be isolated from the rest of the group until parents arrive to prevent the spread of illness. Parents' quick response at such a time also meets the emotional needs of the child who is sick and needing her parents.

Without a note from the pediatrician stating that the child can safely return to group care, a child who has been ill with a fever will not be allowed to return to the center until twenty-four hours have passed without fever.

These simple guidelines met the regulatory requirements our program was responsible for observing, which included a law that all parents be informed by a prominently posted notice of the occurrence of any communicable illness in the center.

Any parent who brings their sick child to school, relying on fever-reducing medicine given at home to mask the symptoms of illness in an attempt to avoid the inconvenience of a sick child, will ultimately be found out. Such behavior on the parent's part is selfish and reckless. Illness can spread to other children, affecting more families, causing an even broader outbreak of illness with its accompanying lost work time. The parent who does not cooperate with reasonable rules regarding disease prevention will be asked to make other arrangements.

> ANY PARENT WHO RELIES ON FEVER-REDUCING MEDICATION TO MASK SYMPTOMS OF ILLNESS WILL BE FOUND OUT.

Children with chronic illness such as diabetes, allergies, or kidney ailments should have a doctor's authorization to be in group day care. The center will be kept advised of any dietary limitations in writing, and parents assist center staff in maintaining the proper diet.

Medications

Some child development programs are willing to administer certain medications to children who do not have communicable illness, for the convenience of their working parents. Parents who need this service must cooperate in meeting their center's procedures in providing this care.

Procedures are established designating how medications are handled and stored, who will administer the doses, and the extent of contemporaneous documentation. The center may decide it is willing to administer certain medicines but not others that might carry more significant risks to children.

Parents note dosing instructions on a medication sheet posted in each classroom. Teachers record the time the medicine is given as well as any noted side effects, and initial the sheet. Any time your child shows any unusual symptoms, you should be called immediately. This includes symptoms related to the illness or side effects to any medication.

Meals, snacks, and foods from home

When centers do not have on-site meal preparation and children bring lunch boxes, policies will be established to avoid candy and other sugary treats. Some state regulations even prohibit this. These foods attract a lot of attention and can diminish other children's experiences during the day. Sugary treats should not be a routine part of any child's diet at school and can be medically dangerous for certain children with whom the child might decide to share.

Meal and snack times occur at specific times each day. You will be informed when your child will be served lunch and snacks. Centers that prepare meals on-site may ask you to call if you're going to be late bringing your child in to the center so the cook will know how to prepare for your child's lunch.

Toys from home

Except for special stuffed animal friends or soft dolls used at naptime, centers usually have policies against children bringing toys from home. There are several good reasons why.

Toys that are safe in the home environment are often unsafe in the more intensive use of center play. Many of the toys purchased by good day care programs come from school supply houses and are designed to withstand more intense use over time. They are manufactured differently from many toys available at discount retailers or department stores. Some of those toys could literally come apart in a typical toddler or preschool classroom. So, except on occasions such as a special "show-and-tell" period, toys from home usually won't be allowed.

Certain "superhero" toys and accessories can lead to superhero conflicts among friends. Your child may love these toys at home, but for young children just developing their social skills, these toys can become quite dangerous. Furthermore, it is part of the young child's nature to sometimes have fuzzy lines between fantasy and reality. We need to avoid anything that could inadvertently encourage a child to harm another while pretending to rule the world.

There is a lot to do and explore in a high-quality preschool program. If a child walks in with a fantastic toy other children wish they had, the whole morning can become about that one toy. While children fuss and cry over having a turn with a life-size doll, this unnatural focus causes them to miss out on other important opportunities for fun and growth.

Outdoor play

Expect your child to participate in morning and afternoon outdoor play periods each day, except on rainy days or when extreme weather conditions arise. Center policies may remind parents to dress children in comfortable, washable clothing, appropriate to the weather conditions. Sometimes busy parents forget to check weather forecasts, and changing weather conditions may require sweaters or coats, hats, and mittens.

When children fully enjoy their outdoor play, they often get dirty. Caregivers help wash hands and faces when children go back into their classroom and may do so at pick-up time, when needed. Some programs are glad to change your child into a clean outfit, brought from home that morning, in preparation for a doctor appointment or dinner out.

Change of clothing

Preschool children who are toilet trained, even pre-k children, can become so engrossed in their activities at times that toileting accidents occur. Most centers ask parents to leave a complete change of clothing in their child's cubby to avoid embarrassment if this should happen.

Parent/staff relations

The director and your caregivers should always be available to discuss or resolve any issue related to your child. Staff members set aside time for phone or in-person meetings when needed. They will provide a substitute for your child's caregiver(s) to participate, if necessary.

A good program will expect all caregivers to interact with parents in a respectful manner and will expect the same of parents at all times. How can children learn kindness and respect toward others if their adult role models can't seem to manage it? In times of difficulty or conflicting opinions, children are best served when everyone handles these kinds of challenges thoughtfully.

Center management should provide time and privacy for staff and parents to meet to address any serious concerns or to resolve a problem. Whether it is a personality conflict, a problem with the child, or a disagreement on what approach to take in a given matter, children should never be present during the conflict-resolution process. It is a mistake to talk about a child as if he cannot hear while he is standing nearby, listening. Adults should find ways to support one another's mutual goals for the child without the child present until the matter is resolved.

> CENTERS JUGGLE THE COMPETING NEEDS TO PAY STAFF WELL WHILE KEEPING TUITION PAYMENTS ACCESSIBLE.

Expect a scheduled parent/teacher conference at least twice per year. The goal will be to discuss your child's developmental progress and to define ways the program can be adjusted to best support your child's development in any area of concern.

Discipline

A good center policy statement will directly address the subject of discipline. Appropriate disciplinary practices with young children are so important to parents and caregivers that we can't overstate the value of taking time to think this issue through thoroughly. You must be sure that you agree with your program's approach to discipline. It is very important that spanking or any physical punishment not occur in any child care program.

The center may state its policy regarding the potential removal of a child who repeatedly demonstrates that he cannot submit to his teacher's authority. On the rare occasion this happens, after parents and staff have worked patiently together to help the child follow simple, reasonable rules about not hurting himself, his friends, or the things we all share, it may be necessary for these parents to find another arrangement. Perhaps this child has not yet developed the typical level of maturity expected at his age. The larger program may be overwhelming this child, and his behavior may be telling us he would be more comfortable in a smaller, less-structured program.

In other cases, a preschool child may have real emotional difficulties that need specialized intervention. Some children with relatively mild difficulty in this area can be effectively integrated into the classroom. In other cases, the typical benefits of the program are lost on a child in this situation. At the same time, continuing out-of-bounds behavior can have significant, negative effects on this child and other children's ability to have an optimal experience, or even to be safe.

Centers can refer parents of this child to programs that provide expert help. Parents are naturally upset if their child must be removed from a program for behavioral reasons. But early intervention provides a much better outcome than delaying it would.

STAFF TURNOVER

It is important for parents to know center policies regarding staff turnover. Turnover is a reality in any program, including those of very high quality. People get married and move away. They decide to go back to school to finish their degree. They develop fatigue and need a change of pace.

Any caregiver change can have a big impact on your child. A good program seeks to minimize the negative impact and emphasize the positive: as one caring adult friend leaves their classroom, another new friend takes her place. Gaining another kind and reliable adult friend has a positive, counterbalancing effect on a child's loss. Even so, everyone works hard to avoid this kind of change happening too often. Unfortunately, programs deal with a variety of issues affecting this hard reality that can be simply beyond their control.

Because child care is labor-intensive, the cost of quality care for children is expensive. Programs struggle to balance tuition accessibility for families against the competing need to pay staff well enough to recruit and retain good caregivers.

Many of our best caregivers stayed with our program for several years but ultimately had to leave for jobs that paid more. Some of these preschool teachers eventually went to work for private or public schools. Other caregivers stayed only a year, leaving at the ideal time for such a change when change is necessary: when their children were promoted to the next age group.

At times a caregiver experiences burnout. The intense demands of the job sometimes overwhelm her, and she must have some time away. Often, the caregiver herself may not recognize she is in this position. And directors and other staff will notice before parents do. It can happen to a director, too. There were several times when my husband insisted on a "leave of absence" for me for this very reason.

Unfortunately, sometimes a director must make the difficult decision to end a staff member's employment. This can happen for a variety of reasons. The staff member may persist in a serious violation of center policies that could place children at risk of harm, such as habitual tardiness, jeopardizing the center's adult/child ratios. Or an individual may be engaging in gossip; the strife that gossip generates can have a terrible effect on the classroom atmosphere, inevitably diminishing the effectiveness of the program. Typically, when a staff member violates staff policies, she doesn't talk about it with parents, so they are not aware of a serious problem.

The director of a good program will do everything within her power to sustain the relationships in the program, and especially those of caregiver to child. These relationships are "where the rubber meets the road" in the program, and protecting them is one of the director's highest goals.

Everyone on a center staff should work together to make any staff transition as smooth as possible for the children affected. In everyone's ideal world, when a staff change occurs, the "old" teacher and the "new" teacher overlap each other in the classroom for a week or two. This allows children to meet their new teacher in a relaxed way and learn that their old teacher likes and approves of her. They also discover that the rules don't change when a new teacher comes in, and this is reassuring. In optimal circumstances, the "old" teacher will come back for a visit from

> PROTECTING RELATIONSHIPS IS ONE OF THE DIRECTOR'S HIGHEST GOALS.

time to time. We were fortunate in our program to do this often. Parents should understand, however, that in the real world, circumstances are not always ideal.

Staff turnover is one of the greatest challenges any center faces. Even when programs have verbal or written contract agreements with staff members, as our program did, life happens. And sometimes individuals make personal choices that can impact centers very negatively. When this happens, the issues affecting a program's ability to find the right personnel quickly are many and varied. Often, there are systemic labor problems affecting an entire business community. Program directors are intrinsically motivated to find the best replacement possible, as quickly as they can, not only for the well-being of children, but also for the best interest of center staff.

Policies for Parents of Infants

Your center will probably have a special set of infant-specific policies. These will include how parents and staff communicate with each other on babies' schedules, sleep times, and feedings. You should see indications that these caregivers appreciate the highly individualized needs of infants in each of these areas.

Centers usually do not provide infant foods and formula. Parents bring these from home. Health departments typically have rules governing how these foods are handled.

Mothers who are breastfeeding should be welcome to bring in their milk in bottles or to stop in to nurse their child. Staff should have very flexible policies to meet your needs in this area.

You should expect to receive a daily report on your baby's day, informing you of significant matters, including how she slept, how she ate, her level of contentment or discontent, diaper changes, and other occurrences. A good program plans for this report to be only a foundation of shared daily information. They'll want you to take time to talk in person with your child's primary caregiver every day, as a matter of routine.

As a new mom, you will want to know you are free to see your baby whenever you like. And from time to time you will notice another mom in the nursery enjoying a visit with her baby and the staff. You can look forward to times like these, too. But during your initial adjustment to this new way of life, you and your baby will probably do better if you wait awhile before you begin midday visits. After all, the separation can be difficult for mom and baby, so repeating it as little as possible in the beginning will hasten your and your baby's adjustment to life in the center nursery.

Policies for parents of toddlers

Policies for toddlers' parents will address some of the challenging behaviors that are a normal part of a toddler's life. You will be informed of how such behaviors are dealt with in the center.

The center should communicate specific ways they manage a toddler's behavior when he is having difficulty. Their philosophy on discipline specific to the very young child should be clear. You should see evidence that they understand how to redirect a toddler's behavior away from a problem area to some new interesting thing to see or do. Toddler caregivers will provide a supportive, friendly, and activities-rich environment. This environment, coupled with toddlers' short attention spans, will make up the largest part of their toddler behavior management plan.

7

WHO'S WATCHING OUT FOR YOU?
LICENSING, RATINGS & ACCREDITATION

Iris James smiled as she watched the children in our threes' class engaged in their morning activities. They had just finished their snack of raisin toast and milk, and since it was misting rain, they would not be going out to play right now. Instead, two small boys were headed to the block center, where they began building a hospital—complete with people figures, cars, and an ambulance.

Two girls and a boy were in the dramatic play center, set up by their caregiver to reflect this week's theme, "A Visit to the Hospital." These three were participating in their own imagined hospital experience. One of the dolls was very ill and needed to see her doctor, who was busy opening her "doctor bag," while her colleague donned his white lab coat. The concerned mother held her baby doll close, wrapped carefully in a blanket, explaining to the doctors that her baby had sniffles and a high fever.

One young artist was disinterested in the morning's circle time discussion of hospitals and health care workers, choosing instead to use paintbrush, watercolors, and easel to create something beautiful.

Another child had been given a brief time-out for hitting her classmate. The look of defiance on her face began to fade as she strained to hear what her teacher was saying to the little boy who was still crying. Shortly, Ms. Rosa Lynn called her over to the table, where she talked with both children about the importance of remembering to use our words when we feel angry and of being kind to our friends.

Iris, an experienced preschool teacher, recognized that the children in this class were doing just what they needed to be doing. They were all appropriately involved in activities, which were effectively planned to meet each child's developmental needs. That included the two who had gotten into a scrape over who got to feed the goldfish today.

Iris had recently resigned her position in a program where she had worked for several years. The center had just been sold, and the new owners clearly had different priorities than those of the previous owners. They were routinely going beyond lawful enrollment capacity in each classroom. Since this change, Iris often found herself responsible for more children in her class than she could properly supervise. She sometimes had had one or two more children above the state's requirements added to her class "just for today." The stress of this situation brought her to us.

OVER THE YEARS THAT I PROVIDED CHILD DAY CARE services, I hired quite a number of employees. We always valued finding someone who met our basic criteria for employment and brought some good experience with her. It was surprising how often I met applicants who were leaving a program because they had been routinely required to supervise too many children.

Requirements for lawfully operating a child care center vary widely from state to state, and in certain states even among individual cities and counties. Some states exempt certain types of programs from the licensing process. And when programs are licensed, many parents assume that they maintain high standards each day. Unfortunately, that is not the case. Even among states that establish higher licensing requirements, it is unlikely that any state regulating agency has sufficient resources to identify and remedy every rule violation. Sometimes unscrupulous providers deliberately attempt to skirt the rules for their own profit or convenience. And violations resulting from human error can occur as dedicated but overloaded directors work within the "muchness" and "manyness" of day care.

> REQUIREMENTS FOR OPERATING A CHILD CARE CENTER LAWFULLY VARY WIDELY FROM STATE TO STATE.

THE NECESSITY OF REGULATION

All regulations related to obtaining a license to operate a child care center are very important and must be diligently upheld to protect the health, safety, and well-being of your child. Parents need to be informed about these rules to help monitor a program's regulatory compliance. Through the department charged with licensing and regulating—overseeing—child care programs, you can obtain information about the regulations that govern child care centers in your state.

Typically, the persons who establish child care regulations and those charged with monitoring centers' compliance with the rules are committed to protecting the well-being of young children. While directors of child care centers may complain at times that certain rules are cumbersome—sometimes, they are—the fact is they are designed to protect. Your program's director may have a summary of these rules available for parents.

States recognize the complexity and significance of this work and provide for routine regulatory oversight. First the regulating agency makes sure that programs applying for an operating license achieve the established standards for license eligibility. Then they check periodically to determine that licensed centers maintain these required standards of practice over time.

Each state has its own requirements, such as how many infants may be supervised by one adult, or how many children are allowed in a particular classroom space. In Tennessee, the Department of Human Services is the primary regulating agency for child care programs. Your state probably has a similar regulating agency. The primary agency coordinates with other regulatory agencies, such as the fire and health departments, to periodically inspect the function of the various services provided.

When parents have some understanding of the legal obligations of their child's center, they can be more effective in helping to monitor the center's compliance with the law. It is reasonable and fair for parents who notice a possible rule violation to speak with the program director. The director of a quality program is always watching to ensure that every aspect of her program conforms to regulations at all times. However, because she cannot be everywhere at all times, she will appreciate that you have brought your concern to her. She may already be aware of a problem and be involved in correcting it. Or this may be new information for her, and you will observe her immediate responsiveness and action to correct the issue.

PARENTS HELP MONITOR A CENTER'S COMPLIANCE.

Regulating agencies make unannounced visits to centers in order to confirm programs' compliance with their regulations. However, each agency is limited in how frequently they are able to visit. Parents need to be watchful, too. These agencies desire and need input from parents when a program disregards the important rules designed to keep children safe. Some states require child development programs to give each parent a summary of state licensing standards upon their child's enrollment in a center.

LICENSING

Centers that are licensed for operation must typically undergo a license renewal process, usually every year. Without renewal, the business or not-for-profit agency cannot continue in operation. You can determine whether a particular program in your area is licensed simply by calling and asking the regulating agency.

Some states require that all for-profit centers must be licensed, but exempt certain not-for-profits, such as church or government funded centers.

If you encounter a program you believe is attempting to operate outside the law, avoiding the entire licensing process, you should assume their standards of practice are inadequate to protect your child. You need to ensure that centers you are considering either have valid licenses for operation or valid license exemptions.

I've met many parents who have the misconception that if a center is licensed by the state, then everything there must be fine. The fact is that licensure alone is not an adequate indication that the program will be acceptable to you. As I indicated, there is a broad range of requirements among states. There is also a broad range of quality among licensed centers, so you must look further. Again, even when child care centers and family day homes are regulated by governmental agencies, parents need to be watchful and engaged.

> THERE IS A BROAD RANGE OF QUALITY AMONG LICENSED CENTERS. YOU MUST LOOK FURTHER THAN LEGAL AUTHORITY TO OPERATE.

All licensed centers and family day homes are required to uphold on a daily basis certain basic standards of practice related to each child enrolled. Sometimes they fail. One individual failure may not make any practical difference on a given day, such as forgetting to hand you your preschooler's daily report, letting you know how she slept at naptime, and how much she ate for lunch. However, certain individual failures could be catastrophic, such as a caregiver forgetting to return a child's medication to a locked container immediately after dosing him at the appointed time.

People are human and human beings make mistakes. So you must be vigilant, too, observing daily that those who protect your child are always focused, including at those times of day when they seem to be just relaxing with children. Professionalism requires that a caregiver be able to relax and enjoy the company of the children she's responsible for while also being aware of and responsive to anything that could harm them.

GOING BEYOND THE BASICS—RATINGS AND ACCREDITATION
Star ratings

Some states are seeking ways to increase quality services for children and are implementing star rating systems to improve parents' ability to assess which programs are high quality. A recent article in the Wall Street Journal reports that fourteen states have implemented star rating plans, the child care equivalent to hotel and restaurant rating systems. About two dozen more states are investigating ways to become involved.[1]

Most states with rating systems in place allow programs to participate voluntarily. Centers that are confident their program goes beyond basic requirements for licensure may choose to undergo a more comprehensive assessment of their professional practice. As states work their way through these new rating systems, sometimes requirements change. For example, a portion of Tennessee's star rating system, which began as a voluntary evaluation, is now mandatory for all licensed centers. Each state establishes which assessment tool they will use to rate their programs. Results are published so the public may access this information to assist in their search for quality day care programs.

The rating system in our state is based, in part, on the Environment Rating Scales developed by the early childhood experts associated with the Frank Porter Graham Child Development Center at the University of North Carolina.[2] Their valuable work deserves great credit for improving the lives of so many young children in day care. Certain other states and municipalities are also using this instrument as a basis for evaluating their programs.

The Environment Rating Scales address various areas of institutional functioning. We are accustomed to thinking of the environment in terms of the natural world. But this instrument evaluates all of the day-to-day experiences affecting your child in day care, encompassing the entire environment provided for children in a given center. It includes the outdoor areas surrounding the building, such as the playground, but goes far beyond this. Evaluation is also made of all safety and health-related issues, as well as staff qualifications and training, curriculum, staff/parent communications, staff/child relationships, and many other areas of concern.

> EACH STATE ESTABLISHES WHICH ASSESSMENT TOOL THEY WILL USE TO RATE THEIR PROGRAMS.

The importance of quality services in each of the areas affecting your child cannot be overstated. After all, we now understand that the first five years of life, the time when most American preschoolers spend some or many of their waking hours in the care of people other than their parents, are so influential. Therefore, you want all the influences that affect your child during this critical period to be the very best, whether at home with you or in a child care program.

Accreditation

There are several national organizations that accredit child development programs. Each of these accrediting agencies has its own set of standards by which acceptable practice is measured. While they may differ in their requirements for accreditation, they have certain goals in common. Accrediting agencies plan to recognize and publicly acknowledge programs that have high standards of professional practice. Through this process, they understand that programs that do not offer these higher-quality services will experience pressure to improve their quality of services to children and families. Inevitably, more and more centers will work to improve quality of care.

> AN ACCREDITED OR HIGHLY RATED PROVIDER HAS VOLUNTARILY ACHIEVED SIGNIFICANTLY MORE DEMANDING STANDARDS THAN A BASIC OPERATING LICENSE REQUIRES.

Accreditation is a voluntary process. Unlike Tennessee's rating system, which is funded by the state government, programs seeking to obtain accreditation must typically pay a fee to the accrediting agency for their services.

A program deciding to enter the accreditation process is informed of the precise standards of professional practice required by the particular accrediting agency. This agency will work with the program over time to conform with these higher standards. When a program has been accredited, just as in Tennessee's star rating system, parents can be assured that this program has met and upholds significantly more demanding standards than those required for a basic operating license.

OTHER REGULATORY OVERSIGHT AGENCIES

In addition to the primary regulating agency in your state, there are other state and local agencies that regulate and oversee your child's program. Parents should understand that no regulating agency can keep watch over any single program every day. And the individual people who inspect your program are capable of missing something. They make mistakes just like the rest of us. It is important to be alert to any obvious dangers that could affect your child or others. Again, a good program's staff stays busy with many responsibilities and will appreciate your bringing to their attention any such concern.

The Fire Department

In Tennessee, the state's fire marshal must approve the building that is to house a child development program. The fire marshal is responsible for upholding both state and federal fire safety standards for child care center buildings.

Buildings must be constructed of acceptable materials. The thickness of walls is addressed, as well as the burn rate of any carpeting or other fabrics. Rooms housing furnaces must be free of any flammable materials. Using stairs with more than a step or two is a challenge for very young children, so exits from their classrooms must not depend on the use of a staircase. The number and location of all exits from the building must meet applicable standards.

Fire extinguishers will be available in designated areas and maintained in readiness. Exits must be marked with lighted exit signs. Just as in a public theater, child care center building exits must also be kept free from any blockage that would prevent a quick exit in case of fire. Periodically, the fire department's inspector will stop in unannounced to ensure that standards are being maintained.

The Health Department

The health department establishes standards for child care centers, too. These include standards for food service and other health-related issues such as sanitation.

If your center has a kitchen, the health department kitchen inspector will stop in periodically to grade the kitchen's safety. They want to ensure that food is being handled, stored, and served in ways that prevent food contamination. Pots and pans, utensils, and dishes must be washed and sanitized according to their standards. The kitchen must be maintained in cleanliness. In Nashville, the standards by which child care center kitchens are graded are identical to and are graded by the same agency as local commercial kitchens, such as those in our city's hospitals and restaurants.

In addition to kitchen inspections, a health department inspector will examine things like proper functioning of all plumbing fixtures in the building. This includes the temperature of hot water at the sinks used by staff and children. If the water is too hot, children will tend not to use it at all. If water temperature is not comfortable, children's hands won't be properly washed. Toilets must be in good working order. Any little nonflushing potties must be emptied and thoroughly sanitized after each use. There must be adequate soap and paper products kept available.

Another division of the health department periodically checks the health records that centers keep on each child and staff member. This inspector comes in to review the health records of every employee and every child enrolled in the program.

The Codes Administration

Many local jurisdictions require that child care land and buildings, whether existing or new construction, must be approved by a building codes authority before being licensed by the state. This inspection prior to opening for business ensures that the building and grounds are safe for use by young children. Periodically, a professional inspector may stop in to check on the general maintenance and safety of the building, grounds, and equipment.

Doorknobs must work properly. Playground equipment must not have hazards that could harm a child. Thorny bushes must be removed. Any broken glass in a window must be promptly replaced. Indoors, tables and chairs must not have any loose legs or parts that could cause injury. Broken toys must be removed and replaced.

The inspector's safety concerns also include ensuring that the required parking areas and traffic flow plan into and out of the property are maintained as originally approved. Proper outdoor lighting must be provided for the safety of ingress and egress in the early darkness of fall and winter months.

SO WHO'S WATCHING OUT FOR YOU?

It is reassuring to know that government officials and other experts are addressing the important issues affecting young children in out-of-home care. It would be impossible for any parent to evaluate all these areas alone. Yet, the answer to the question above is and must always be—*you*. You must watch out for your child. If you see something that seems wrong, speak up! Your state government and Bill O'Reilly have unique ways they can help look out for you, but no one can take your place when it comes to protecting your little one—no matter how expert or well-intentioned they may be.

In a quality program, the staff will be glad to receive your input about something they might not have noticed. And they will assure you that they are either already addressing the problem or moving forward immediately to resolve it. If your program's staff members do not appreciate your reasonably expressed concern, you have reason to ask yourself—and your provider—why.

PART FOUR

The Tour

INTRODUCTION TO THE TOUR

IN CHAPTER ONE, I SHARED MY MEMORY of a visit to a day care program where children were seriously neglected. The exterior of the facility was also neglected. Obviously, the neglect of maintenance and the neglect of children don't necessarily go hand in hand, however. Children can be wonderfully provided for in a building that is overdue for painting, for example, where staff and parents are holding bake sales and other fund-raisers to earn money to improve their building. And it is possible for children to be seriously neglected in a beautiful facility where everything looks really great. Things are not always as they seem.

When you visit a child care program you are considering, remember to avoid bringing your child with you on your first visit(s), if possible. You need to focus on everything you see and hear...

wayne and Yvonne Gray had enrolled their four-year-old daughter, Monique, in a program that had an excellent reputation. It was known throughout the area for its quality and was very close to their new home. However, while Monique loved her old day care in Atlanta, she was very unhappy in the new one. Dwayne and Yvonne were beginning to have reservations, too.

While everything looked wonderful in the new center, the staff members were not as welcoming as they had expected. The center had just hired a new director, and there was a palpable tension in the air. When the Grays asked another parent whether she sensed anything was wrong, she told them that a lot of staff policies had changed along with the change of directors. The staff was angry and upset. The Grays concluded that this was why Monique's adjustment to this program was such a challenge. She was not receiving the attention and support from her caregivers that any preschool child needs. Because of the uncertainty of how long this might continue, they decided to make the sacrifice of extra drive time to enroll her with us.

EQUIPPING YOU TO RECOGNIZE QUALITY

If you have never toured a good child development center or have never been in one, you're in for a very interesting experience. You are about to enter a whole new world. So it helps to have some idea of what to expect. The purpose of Part Four is to equip you to recognize quality when you see it.

As we consider, one by one, the various aspects of a strong program, I will explain some of the reasons why things are set up the way they are, including in the classrooms and on the playground. Considering the way things work in a good child development program will help you identify certain elements that may be missing in some centers you visit. Ultimately, you may find it necessary to enroll in a program that doesn't have everything you would prefer. But a later section of this book will address ways you, as the parent, are uniquely able to influence any program to work better for your child.

Part Four provides additional information about children's developmental needs at various stages of growth and offers some examples of how a properly structured program meets these needs. As we walk through the program together, you will come to better understand how different elements of a good program affect your child.

I will also help you to identify some quality indicators in every area of the program, from food service to emergency planning, from daily schedules to book corners. And Part Four will lay a foundation for what to look for in appropriate person-to-person interactions, including adult-to-child, child-to-child, and adult-to-adult interactions in the presence of children.

Introduction to The Tour

TAKE TIME TO SEE EVERYTHING—THE PLEASANT AND THE NOT-SO-PLEASANT

Your tour should be relaxed and unhurried. Ideally, the director, the assistant director, or whoever is accompanying you on the tour will allow you to take your time and really absorb everything these children are experiencing. If a fight breaks out in the three-year-old class, steel your heart and stand your ground! Don't shrink back from this difficult situation because of dread that your child might actually have to face something like this one day without you right there to protect him. He almost certainly will have to face this one day, because it is a normal part of growing up. And you now have a valuable opportunity to see how this conflict is resolved. You need to know that resolution takes place in a way that you support if your child were involved—and in a good program, it will be. You will be encouraged when you see how a skillful preschool teacher turns this tough situation into an opportunity for growth for each child involved.

Your host or hostess should make you welcome and should be interested in answering every question you ask. The time this takes will vary and is obviously impacted by the program's size and the physical space it occupies. After your initial tour in a center you like, it is ideal to return for a full day or morning, or some longer period of time. You'll want to be certain your first impressions prove accurate.

PREPARING YOU TO CHOOSE THE RIGHT CENTER FOR YOUR FAMILY

As you visit various centers on your short list, you may see one that has many of the qualities you're looking for but lacks one aspect that is very important to you. In another center, you may find the desired characteristic missing from the first program, but it may lack other important things. The point is, don't expect perfection. Even if you find a center that seems perfect, don't expect it to be that way every day.

Remember that even at home we can't maintain perfection. Be realistic in your expectations and know that as you go through the search process, you will become increasingly clear about what is important to you for your child. Then when you see the right program, you'll recognize it.

8

THE NEIGHBORHOOD, BUILDING AND GROUNDS

rom the moment Edith and Delbert Jones stepped into my office and sat down, I knew something serious had happened to them. Edith was quiet but was unable to stop the flow of tears streaming down her face. Delbert's hands were shaking. This couple had obviously been frightened by something. They had just come from their child's day care center and had decided they would not be taking her back. Their daughter Mary was, at the moment, safely with their next-door neighbor, a longtime family friend, until they could make another arrangement.

Although I was not personally convinced at first that the move they were making was necessary, I certainly understood their position. The program they were leaving was highly regarded, and their child had been very happy and content there. I listened as Delbert explained what had happened.

At about eleven o'clock that morning, Delbert had received a call at his office from the center's assistant director. She called to let him know of an incident that had just occurred.

The playground of Mary's center was situated across a public street from its main building. Teachers routinely had to traverse this normally quiet roadway with groups of young children, going to and from the playground. This morning, as Mary's class was returning from their outdoor play period to begin preparing for lunch, a motorcycle sped across their path. Although no one was harmed, the teacher was badly shaken and the children in the group were startled and frightened. Some needed the comfort and presence of their parents, including Mary.

Mr. and Mrs. Jones explained that, before enrolling Mary, they were concerned that she would be crossing that street, but the benefits of the program otherwise persuaded them to set this concern aside. Mary had been very happy there for the past year. While her parents knew this was probably just an isolated incident, they were not willing to take the risk that it could happen again.

IN TENNESSEE, THE PROCESS OF LICENSING A CHILD development center requires meeting many standards related to the building that houses the program as well as the grounds surrounding it. While states' regulating agencies periodically check to ensure their required standards are being maintained, some of these standards of acceptability may not meet your standards. Therefore, you must observe carefully and think about what you see.

THE NEIGHBORHOOD

Safety

On the day you tour a center, the first thing you must pay attention to is the neighborhood it is in. Most centers want to be conveniently located, because they understand what an important consideration this is for families choosing a program. But governmental approval of a particular location may have more to do with traffic flow or zoning than with neighborhood safety. And sometimes, due to financial constraints, programs must choose a location that is less than ideal.

If you really like everything you see in this center but are concerned about neighborhood safety, consider calling the police department to find out about crime in that area. Is there a history of crime that has impacted this center? What kinds of businesses are nearby? Do these businesses pose potential problems? Think about whether you would feel safe being in this area with your child during the times of year when the days are short and it will be dark outside at drop-off and pick-up times.

Proximity to Emergency Services

Consider the location of the program in relation to emergency services. How close is the nearest hospital, and does it have specialized emergency services for young children? Where is the nearest fire department? How long would EMS take to arrive and transport a seriously ill or injured child? While it is unlikely that your child will ever need these services, knowing they're close just in case provides peace of mind. Good proximity to emergency services could leave you favoring one program over another if the decision between two providers could otherwise go either way.

Noise Pollution and Other Hazards

What about sources of noise pollution? A location situated within a block or so of a fire department or a hospital is an obvious benefit in case of emergency. However, being that close may mean that naptimes will be regularly interrupted by loud sirens. A nearby expressway or railroad will also be noisy. And a nearby airport may mean that the center is under the flight path of planes all day.

> THE CENTER MAY BE IN A LOVELY NEIGHBORHOOD, BUT THE DEVELOPMENT GOING IN NEXT DOOR COULD BE A PROBLEM.

The center you are visiting may be in a lovely neighborhood, but that beautiful new commercial or residential real estate development going in right next door could be a problem. There may be a lot of dust and heavy-equipment exhaust fumes, or in the case of a large commercial construction project, jackhammers or blasting. Issues like these could really have a negative impact on children's playground experiences, or possibly even on their indoor hours—including naptime. Real estate development projects can take years to complete, and problems like these could affect a significant portion of your child's preschool experience.

Think about anything in a center's neighborhood that could have a negative impact on young children.

THE BUILDING AND GROUNDS

First impressions

When you see a center from the street for the first time, whether it is a large child development program or a residence housing a family day home, what is your initial impression? Does it appeal to you, or does it leave you feeling a little uncomfortable? If you're uncomfortable, try to define exactly why. There's no need to make a judgment about a given program based solely on first impressions, especially if you've heard a good report from a credible source; but you should be aware of what you're feeling.

Does the building appear well maintained? Is an effort made to provide some attractive landscaping, and is it well kept? Building and grounds maintenance is a challenge in any child care center because of the intensive nature of its use, but it is important. If the lawn has more weeds than grass or the hedges are badly overgrown, or litter and other debris are all over the place, this may indicate that something more is wrong. The budget may be stretched too thin to hire people to do this work. If the building looks as though it's been way too long since it was painted, that may likewise indicate a budgetary problem. It's okay to ask. After all, there may be a reasonable explanation for why building maintenance has fallen behind. The staff may have a plan to address maintenance needs. But such problems could be symptoms of inadequate funding, and this otherwise acceptable program might not provide the long-term solution you need.

Is the interior space inviting?

Does the entrance area seem welcoming for parents and children? Are the common areas of the interior—including the office(s), kitchen, teacher resource areas, and restrooms—well maintained, orderly, and kept reasonably clean? Does it appear that whatever dust or dirt is visible has been there no more than a day or so, indicating a janitorial service is under contract in a large center or that it is cleaned regularly by someone in a small program? Is the center's license posted prominently as required by law? Is a health department rating likewise posted? What does it say? Do any regulatory postings indicate anything pending or probationary about the status of services by this provider? Do you see an attractive and helpful bulletin board for parents containing current postings, giving evidence of the staff's concern for parents and opportunities for parental involvement?

> DO ANY REGULATORY POSTINGS REQUIRED BY LAW INDICATE ANYTHING PENDING OR PROBATIONARY?

Can you see into all classrooms?

Do the doors opening into individual classrooms have windows that allow you a clear line of sight into the space? French doors help adults entering the room see whether a small child is on the other side before opening the door. This can prevent accidentally bumping into a child. Additionally, such doors provide feelings of openness and spaciousness. This encourages support and friendship among staff members, in addition to keeping them accountable to one another.

ARE THE BUILDING AND GROUNDS A COMMUNITY ASSET?

You should feel at ease and comfortable here. Perfection is not necessary, realistic, or even desirable, for that matter. But the overall appearance of the building, both exterior and interior, as well as the grounds, should at least be consistent with the community of which it is a part and should be an appealing asset to that community.

THE PLAYGROUND

BASIC PLAYGROUND STRUCTURE

As you enter the parking area, notice the location of the playground. Does it have adequate, well-maintained fencing? Is there an entrance to it directly from a public area, and, if so, is this gate kept locked to restrict access?

Is the space visually appealing for children, inviting them to come and play? Does the playground have any large trees that will provide shady play areas in the summer? If not, are canopies provided?

> PLAYGROUNDS THAT ADJOIN THE BUILDING AFFORD SAFE, DIRECT ACCESS.

Most preschool playgrounds adjoin the building housing the center. This affords safe, direct access for teachers and children. Except for extreme weather conditions, children will use the playground every day, usually for some time both in the mornings and in the afternoons. Safe access is definitely important.

If the playground does not adjoin the building, is it located across a public street? Some states allow centers to use such an arrangement. But how much traffic is on that street at different times of the day? Would a teacher supervising a group of young children always be able to cross safely?

Regulatory agencies require more square footage per child outside than inside. This acknowledges children's natural need to play and move differently outdoors and allows for plenty of space for these kinds of activities. Some programs use the minimum space allowed by the regulations. Does this playground seem to have plenty of room for those times when several classes of children might be out playing at the same time?

Why the playground is so important

The playground will be very important to your child, for many of the same reasons why she loves to play in your backyard or at the park. Preschool children need to run, jump, climb, and try lots of new physical challenges, such as catching a ball or sliding down a sliding board. Younger children need to push and pull toys around and toddle from place to place in a larger space than a classroom can provide. These activities are really fun for the young child, and all healthy children love this kind of play.

But there's a lot more going on here. When children play outdoors, they get the fresh air and sunshine their bodies need. At the same time, they are developing strength and control of the large muscles in their bodies. They are becoming more agile and less likely to fall as young toddlers often do. Thinking about the differences between the way an adult moves and walks compared to the movements of a young child, it is easy to understand why children are so active and love to run and play so much—it allows their bodies to develop as they grow toward adulthood.

Playground equipment needs

You should find a good variety of well-maintained, developmentally appropriate equipment on the center's playground, including various structures for climbing up and over and through. Young children also need outdoor playhouses where impromptu "club meetings" and other types of dramatic play can occur. Large, soft beach balls for safe throwing should be available. Paved tricycle and three-wheeler tracks are important, too, as are sand and water tables. Outdoor art stations provide a restful break from more vigorous activity for children who want to move away from the action. Planting a small flower or vegetable garden in springtime, playing in sprinklers in summer, and raking leaves in fall are fun for everyone. Good options for safe outdoor play are pretty much endless, and a creative staff will provide many choices.

> ANY AREAS WHERE A CHILD COULD FALL FROM A PIECE OF EQUIPMENT MUST HAVE A SOFT, RESILIENT SURFACE UNDERNEATH.

Any areas where a child could fall from a piece of equipment must have a thick layer of soft, resilient material, such as sand, mulch, or river gravel to cushion a fall. Sufficient distance between large, stationary equipment will reduce the risk of children colliding with each other or the equipment when running on the playground.

Choices and conflicts

Preschoolers should have plenty of opportunities to choose their play on the playground. Sometimes as children make these choices, conflicts will arise. Who got to the red tricycle first? "I did!" "No, I did!" These experiences provide opportunities for children to grow and develop socially and emotionally. It is fascinating to watch how they find ways to work these things out. Fierce emotions and emphatic statements like, "I'm not your friend anymore!" soon yield to peaceful coexistence as their interest in the tricycle fades when someone suggests a pretending game that requires more than one participant. Then they're off to something entirely different.

Occasionally children need a teacher's intervention to prevent any harm when someone is very upset. This is where teachers help children learn conflict resolution, kindness, and respect for friends. Reminders to "use our words when we feel angry" provide additional opportunities to help children develop language skills and emotional control.

Playgrounds for every age and stage

Two-year-olds need their own playground for several reasons. They're quite a lot bigger than younger toddlers and are much more agile. But they're no match for the physical skills of the older preschoolers. Even though they enjoy watching the older children sometimes, if allowed to enter that playground without very close-at-hand supervision, they could quickly become overwhelmed. They need their own playground where life moves at a two-year-old pace, for the same reason babies and younger toddlers must be protected from the twos.

Older babies and young toddlers need outdoor time, too, with age-appropriate equipment for them, including some infant/toddler swings, toys for pushing and pulling, and other colorful toys and balls. Infant classes and toddler classes should be separated from each other on the playground. And, of course, their play space is set apart from older preschoolers' outdoor play area. Older preschoolers move much too fast for them, and the equipment those children use would be dangerous for tiny people.

You will notice that as they develop, young toddlers begin to play alongside their friends. They don't interact with each other much, but getting used to playing beside someone familiar to them is a precursor to the social interaction that will come a little later. The larger space of the playground is a good, nonthreatening place for this kind of experience.

It is ideal, too, for the young toddler to do his most important work—learning to walk better and moving objects from here to there.

Caregivers and Playgrounds: Relaxed, Focused, and Involved

When it's time to take the children out to play, the change of scene can be a relief for everyone. Because the larger space of the outdoors relieves certain stresses of the indoor experience for children, caregivers can expect to relax a little outdoors, too. Just as a small town often has a more relaxed pace than a big city, going outdoors relieves some of the pressures of population density. Conflicts can arise among children just because of the closeness of indoor classroom space. Going out benefits staff, too, but this does not mean caregivers take a break from involvement with children. They remain engaged with them through conversation, as well as offering to read a book or provide art materials outdoors. Staff members maintain constant watch over every move every child makes on the playground.

> ADULT CONVERSATION MUST NEVER DISTRACT FROM CAREGIVERS' PRIMARY RESPONSIBILITY—PROTECTING THE CHILDREN.

Staff members must position themselves throughout the playground in such a way as to compensate for any barriers that obscure proper visual monitoring of child activity. If teachers are all seated in a small area, who is watching the child behind the tree? Monitoring the children's play must be facilitated both by where teachers are seated, whenever they do sit down for a moment, and by walking around among and visiting with the children.

Caregivers enjoy adult conversation without distraction

On beautiful days, a few classes of three- to five-year-old preschoolers may share the playground. The teachers in these classes may not have had much time to see one another for a while and will naturally want to speak to each other. This is a good thing, because the friendships that form among staff, as well as between staff and parents, can have a very positive impact on all the children. However, professionalism requires that the enjoyment of each other's company must never distract caregivers from their primary responsibility on the playground—protecting the children. A vigilant caregiver is able to prevent many accidents. Distracted child care staff members are unable to exercise the constant watchfulness and quick response that is necessary when monitoring children's outdoor play.

Going outdoors: an orderly transition

When two- through five-year-olds go to their playgrounds each morning and afternoon, it is wise to help them make this transition in an orderly way. While it isn't essential every time, it is good for children to grow accustomed to lining up to go outside like the big boys and girls do. Continuing to use their inside voices while they're still inside and responding to a teacher's request for a few moments of quiet before they walk outside are routines that would serve well if an emergency building evacuation was necessary. This is also an important way to avoid the possibility that children will fall and tumble all over one another, as would happen if they were allowed to just break out of doors, like calves out of a stall. Also, children need to understand very early that concrete is for walking on; playgrounds are for running.

9

THE CLASSROOMS

On the day Maureen McGill stopped by, early in the afternoon on a rainy Monday, I didn't have any appointments scheduled. The phones had been relatively quiet, and after my initial rounds through the classrooms, I enjoyed the leisure of catching up on some simple tasks and leafing through a few professional magazines.

Walking downstairs for a casual visit to Nursery II, I paused in the breezeway for a moment to watch the rain fall. As I turned to open the nursery door, a car drove into our parking lot. An unfamiliar woman stepped out while opening her umbrella and walked briskly toward the building. When she stepped inside, she introduced herself and shook off the rain, then asked if by any chance we had space for her five-month-old baby boy, Tommy. I invited Maureen to peek in at our young toddlers, who were all sound asleep. Then I asked if she'd like to come upstairs to my office.

Maureen expressed a concern I had heard before. Whenever she stopped by her current day care center at a time other than her regular pick-up time, she found her baby either in his crib or in a swing. The nursery staff of Tommy's day care seemed to be keeping him and the other babies in cribs or swings too much. The hair on the back of his head was thinning—he was developing a little bald spot. Maureen was concerned that being in one position too long might explain why. She also noted that Tommy's development wasn't where she expected him to be and wondered whether limitations on his activity might be influencing this.

Maureen wanted Tommy to be moving around on his own more during the day, and after the staff of his present day care was unresponsive to her concerns, she decided to make a change.

CLASSROOM SPACES IN A CHILD DEVELOPMENT PROGRAM should be bright, cheerful, and inviting. And the way these spaces are set up, along with the activity options they provide, will have a big impact on what your child's day will be like and whether or not he receives certain important developmental support. Here we'll consider the structure of effective classrooms, from the infant nursery to pre-k. And we'll observe how babies, toddlers, and preschoolers use their classrooms and why their personal choices are so important.

THE INFANT NURSERY

The importance of baby's first year

Whether in a child care center or a family day home, babies need specialized care. The importance of the earliest months of life cannot be overstated. The diversity and volume of information babies acquire in their first year is great and will have a critical influence on who this little person will become as an older child and as an adult.

The casual observer of the newborn might conclude that there's not much going on with this little guy, who sleeps most of the time and is nursing, or is demanding to be nursed, when he is awake. Nothing could be farther from the truth! Every single experience this baby has facilitates the development of his brain, which is not fully developed at birth.[1] The stimulus an infant receives or does not receive in the first year can have a profound impact throughout life.

THE APPROPRIATE NURSERY: FACILITATING THE WAY BABIES LEARN

Babies learn through their five senses, so an appropriate environment for infants from birth to twelve months will reflect this. A soft play area with adequate space will be provided so that babies can have freedom of movement. And caregivers will spend a lot of their time on the floor with babies, talking and singing to them, supporting their efforts to try new skills. Caregivers will be sure colorful, textural objects suitable for infants are close by, encouraging babies to reach out, touch, and eventually grasp them. As the infants develop rudimentary eye-hand coordination and strength and control over large and small muscles, these objects will inevitably end up in their mouths. This is good, because babies learn about their world through the feel of objects in the mouth.

> THE INFANT'S BRAIN IS NOT FULLY DEVELOPED AT BIRTH.

In addition to making sure the nursery environment is free of any choking hazards, a good infant caregiver is to be relentless about washing and disinfecting toys every day. Watchful caregivers will systematically ensure that an object that finds its way into a baby's mouth is removed from the play area as soon as the child loses interest in it so it can be sanitized before another can use it.

Caregivers place unbreakable mirrors at a baby's eye level so she can see her own face; this encourages her to try scooting and later crawling over for a look. Simply designed, single-object pictures may be placed at baby height for close examination. And attractive collages and mobiles may be hung up higher to encourage babies' visual exploration.

Babies need to move

Babies will be in their cribs only when falling asleep, napping, or gradually waking up. Even younger babies who are ready will have some time with toys, including musical ones, on a pallet or in an area set aside for this purpose. While the younger infants enjoy this freedom, older, larger babies who are capable of scooting around are carefully kept otherwise engaged to protect the littlest ones. This period on the floor will alternate with limited periods of time in an infant seat or swing, and plenty of time in their primary caregiver's arms or playing beside her on the floor. Caregivers are quick to respond and help babies change position when they no longer express interest or enjoyment.

It is possible to hold babies too little, and it's possible to hold them too much. When held too little, babies miss opportunities to form close attachments and begin basic interaction with others. It's more appealing for them to make their own sounds when someone else is appreciating these along with them. When held too much, they can become too dependent and sometimes inappropriately demanding. This can make it harder for the child to experience contentment within herself, to be able to be comfortable living in her own skin. When the nursery is set up to be really interesting for infants, they won't want to spend too much time in anybody's arms—nor should they, because they would then miss out on other important opportunities to move around and discover new things.

> CAREGIVER INTEREST AND ENCOURAGEMENT HELPS PROTECT AND SUPPORT THE CHILD'S EARLY EFFORTS.

As motor skills develop and infants begin to scoot around on their tummies, to crawl, and to sit up on their own—and eventually pull up, stand, and walk—caregivers will be very close at hand. The caregiver's interest and encouragement helps protect and support the child's early efforts. This also encourages the baby's feeling of competency and pleasure in trying out new skills.

Sounds in the environment

Even when sleeping, babies are influenced by the sounds around them. Exposure to music, and particularly certain classical music, is an important offering for babies. Other soft, melodious music at quiet times of the day, along with fun, bouncy music at more active times, enhance the value of these periods. Whenever possible, the infant will be protected from loud, abrupt sounds that would startle or distress him.

Babies enjoy being spoken to in gentle, melodic tones. The sound of a calm, reassuring human voice is appealing to the very young infant, and this can be seen in the baby's facial expression. Caregivers will use every opportunity to talk and sing to babies throughout their first year: when feeding, changing, rocking, and playing. This encourages focus beyond themselves to the world around them and forms early understandings of human interaction, including the use of language. Just because a baby cannot talk does not mean she cannot understand. The baby is learning continuously, waking or sleeping.

Learning to trust

I believe that trust is one of the most vital developmental needs in the first twelve months of a person's life. The infant whose basic needs are met lovingly, gently, and consistently learns that this new world into which she has come is a good place. When she is hungry and cries, someone feeds her. When she is tense and needs calm, someone holds or rocks her, and she is reassured. In this way, she begins to form positive expectations of the world and the significant persons around her. She also begins to understand how valuable she is and that she can expect to get what she needs in life.

On the other hand, the baby who is handled by an impatient caregiver who responds to her cries with frustration is learning that she must fight in order for her needs to be met and that this always takes difficult and prolonged effort. Her world is not such a happy place when she is left alone in her difficulties. How can the child in this circumstance form fundamentally positive attitudes toward herself and others? I cannot imagine that such visceral psychological conditioning in infancy does not follow a person throughout life. Lessons learned on such a deep level must be an enormous challenge to unlearn later, even into adulthood.

A GOOD NURSERY IS A CALM PLACE

If an infant nursery is properly designed and infant caregivers are properly trained, there will not be a lot of crying. Babies do cry at home, in the car, at the grocery, at grandmother's house, and at day care, and this is normal. How else will they let you know when they're hungry or tired, or when they need changing? Crying is their only language at first. However, when the babies' needs are being appropriately planned for in the center, the amount of crying from each child should be no more than what would be expected in the home, and will often be less. Yes, really! I know this is true, because parents have told me so. I attribute this to the complete orientation to infants' needs in an appropriate child care nursery—more than is possible at home. Family life in the home often requires focus on many issues at the same time, such as the needs of older siblings, preparing dinner, washing laundry, and so on.

> THE INFANT WHOSE NEEDS ARE MET LOVINGLY AND CONSISTENTLY IS LEARNING TO TRUST.

Sleeping/waking/feeding schedules

As a new infant is enrolled into the program, that child will continue her individual at-home sleeping/waking/feeding schedule. No one should attempt to force any baby away from her natural schedule—especially not while the infant is already having to deal with a lot of new experiences. Babies should be fed when they are hungry and allowed to sleep when they are sleepy.

However, as the new infant gradually settles into her new life in the center, she often begins to make some changes on her own. These changes can occur very naturally and subtly over a period of time. Sometimes this happens simply because the child is growing older and needs less naptime and fewer feedings. Such changes would be taking place at home, too. But newly enrolled older infants often make their own schedule changes as well. Very interesting things occur when most of the babies are awake, enjoying music, scooting around on the floor, happily swinging in swings or in caregivers' arms, making their baby sounds and playing with their teachers. The new baby soon finds all these novel sights and sounds fascinating. She naturally wants to observe more and more of this interesting stuff and may delay sleep a little while to indulge her interests.

In a good nursery, blessed by the presence of trained and dedicated caregivers, a very pleasing rhythm of life develops. Caregivers know each child very well and are able to anticipate and prepare for upcoming needs. It's wonderful for caregivers and children on those special days when the baby stars align and everybody sleeps, wakes, and dines over approximately the same intervals.

Sanitation

Caregivers must be constantly vigilant to avoid the spread of germs in a nursery. Children who develop fever, vomiting, diarrhea, or other illnesses while at day care must be isolated until parents can arrive to take them home or to the pediatrician. Parents must protect the other children in the nursery as well as their own child by promptly arriving when called, thereby respecting this need for isolation. Everyone's cooperation is essential to make this system work.

Diapers are changed frequently at a scheduled routine throughout the day and additionally, whenever needed, for each baby. Caregivers are trained to use protective straps or to keep one hand on the baby at all times while changing a diaper to prevent the baby from falling off the changing station. Diaper trash is removed frequently to prevent odors in the nursery.

Hand washing for adults and children is a priority, especially at diaper change time. Caregivers use latex gloves when changing and disposing of diapers and diaper trash. After each use, diaper-changing table surfaces are disinfected with a bleach and water solution, as prescribed by the health department.

MEALTIME ROUTINES

When babies are fed solid infant foods, they are held on laps or, if they are older, seated in infant seats or high chairs designed to prevent tipping over. As caregivers look on, older infants should be allowed to experiment with feeding themselves, using their fingers to pick up some of their green beans or carrots, cut to bite size.

Nursing mothers will be provided rocking chairs in the classroom for nursing or, if they desire more privacy, in a welcoming and comfortable area set apart for this purpose. When caregivers give babies their bottles, they cradle them in their arms for whatever time each child needs. Propping the bottle and leaving a young baby to feed alone for the caregiver's convenience is never acceptable. Older infants who prefer to hold their own bottles will be allowed to do so when parents and caregivers agree they're ready.

Mealtime should be a pleasant experience, and babies must not be rushed. This is an important opportunity for the caregiver to reinforce the child's understanding that she really enjoys the baby's company, and the child learns that eating lunch is a happy time. The baby begins to develop a healthy attitude toward mealtime, food, and her caregiver. Caregivers will wash the baby's hands and face, as well as their own hands, before and after the feeding. High chairs are disinfected after each use.

> PROPPING A BOTTLE AND LEAVING A BABY TO FEED ALONE IS NEVER ACCEPTABLE.

Nursery furnishings and equipment

Nurseries should provide an individual crib for each child, with sheets and blankets that are changed daily—or more often if needed. Parents should be allowed to bring items such as special blankets and mobiles for small babies to look at. Creating a pretty "nest" for their child may be more comforting at first for parents than for babies, but that doesn't make it any less important.

Any hard surface edges, such as those on shelving or changing station cabinetry, should be rounded. Any protruding screws or other potentially harmful hardware on cribs or other infant equipment will be covered with some protective device, such as plastic covers, to prevent harm to a baby who might fall against them. Professional-grade carpet cleaning should occur frequently, and caregivers immediately use smaller cleaning machines to clean and disinfect spills or spit-ups.

In addition to being safe, is the nursery a pleasing atmosphere for infants? Are wall and flooring colors soft and restful? A nursery may have many brightly colored objects, but it's good for these large surface areas to be restful to the eye. Do windows to the outside allow your child to see clouds passing by or rain coming down? Even better, does a window or French door to the outside invite a small person to crawl over, pull herself up, and look out at her eye level whenever she would enjoy a change of scenery?

Is there an emergency exit accessible directly from the classroom? Is the door wide enough for a caregiver to place all of her babies in one crib and roll them right out if they needed to quickly evacuate the room? Do caregivers have to walk far to get to the babies' outdoor play space?

How does this nursery make you feel?

How does this room make you feel as you observe it objectively? Is it kept at a comfortable temperature, not too warm and not too cool? Is the room free of odors that would indicate inadequate sanitation practices? What do you hear in this room? Are caregivers' voices relaxed and appealing? What is it like from a baby's point of view when you move down to their eye level for a look? Is this a calm, friendly place where you would be comfortable spending time? If this space and its setup feel good to you, it will probably feel good to your baby, too.

THE TODDLER ROOM

For our purposes, we define toddlers as those who have begun to walk, or are on the brink of doing so, and who range in age from around twelve to twenty-four months.

The change in equipment meets toddlers' changing needs

Unlike in the nursery, most toddler rooms will not have cribs. Most of these children are still using their cribs at home, of course, but their naptime schedule has changed. They won't miss their cribs as they nap on cots or mats on the floor, which are covered with a clean sheet and blanket. These will be stacked and removed after naptime so that floor space is freed for toddlers' greater need: toddling.

High chairs will be replaced by a low table, with little chairs all around. This is where toddlers will have lunch and make art. In another area will be the diaper-changing station, which continues to be very important, of course. Just as in the infant nursery, caregivers must always keep one hand on the child they are diapering, to protect against a fall.

A restroom will be close by, including a child-height sink where, with a teacher's help, toddlers will wash their hands. There you will also find a bathroom fixture you may never have seen—a very small flushing toilet. Most children don't concern themselves with potty training until they are around two to two and a half, but a few may begin this process early. When the other children notice, they begin to understand that this is something little people can do, just like big people.

Ideally, as in the nursery, child-height windows let toddlers observe the outdoors at their eye level. Also, a door directly to the outside facilitates easy playground access for children for whom walking is still challenging.

How Your Toddler Uses This New Space

This classroom is a very active place. Most of the time, the majority of the little people are moving. The toddler room is set up to accommodate this obvious need. Often the environment is enhanced by child-friendly music. Periodically their teacher(s) will invite some children to come to the table for a simple art activity or to play with a modeling compound. Some join and stay very briefly before they're off again, while others remain engaged a little longer.

Later, all the children may be asked to join their teacher on the floor for circle time, and most of them will sit with her for a song or a story or finger play. This periodic interruption of activities that toddlers would naturally choose on their own has several benefits: Often toddlers listen and participate briefly, intrigued by the way a sensitive caregiver uses her voice in appealing ways during a short presentation. Here they are learning more about the importance of other people and of language, adding a new word or two at times. Additionally, this time gives children a break from the previous more active period. This has a calming effect. Then, when they go back to their play, they are refreshed and their activities seem new again.

> MOST OF THE TIME, MOST OF THE LITTLE PEOPLE ARE MOVING.

Because toddlers' ability to attend is very brief, circle time doesn't last long—often only five to ten minutes or so, and sometimes less, depending on the children's interest. This limited attention span serves an important function: toddlers need to keep moving, because toddlers need to keep learning.

Toys and materials

Lots of toys will be accessible, including duplicates or triplicates of certain very popular toys, thus reducing conflict among the children. Push and pull toys are important at this age but tend to cause less frustration when used in the larger outdoor space. Toddler-safe blocks, including nesting blocks, trucks and cars, and animal and people figures, encourage imaginative play. Other toys encourage eye-hand coordination and small muscle development and control, such as snap-together toys and widemouthed plastic bottles into which smaller toys may be repeatedly inserted and poured out.

Soft floor pillows and washable stuffed animals make a book corner inviting. Here children enjoy developmentally appropriate, colorful, and accessible picture books. In this quieter area, an older child can also work on large, simple puzzles.

A climbing corner of big, vinyl-upholstered shapes forming low steps and slides designed just for toddlers is a valuable provision for this room. Climbing needs are met safely, facilitating large muscle development and control. An indoor dollhouse large enough for children to walk in and out of, and equipped with home-center items such as toy pots and pans, provides a wonderful place for pretending or hiding or peekaboo. And an unbreakable mirror hung on the wall next to a hat rack offers a place for fun and funny experiences.

How Toddlers Use Activity Centers

In the toddler room, the actual function of basic activity centers will probably appear to be at odds with their original intent. You may notice a truck has been left in a doll bed, or someone has abandoned two or three blocks in the book corner. Simple activity centers may be used effectively with toddlers, although not in the same way that older children use them. Toddlers learn where to look for what they want when toys are stored routinely in the same place. They begin to get the sense that there is order to things. But don't expect them to be able to actually keep order.

On most occasions when you visit the toddler room, there will be toys, dolls, some books, and a random shoe or two all over the floor. This is evidence that the toddlers are doing exactly what they're supposed to be doing.

There's no need to expect hats and dolls to stay in the home center. They'll end up wherever the toddler discards them for something else that captures their interest. It's good to remind toddlers from time to time that home center is a good place for pots and pans, because this helps them begin to understand there is a place for things. But rigid enforcement is not appropriate here.

Cleanup time with toddlers

Periodically, soft blocks and trucks will be returned to the block and truck area, and dolls will be returned to their beds. Teachers do this for and with the children by making a game of this routine, usually accompanied by a "cleanup time" song.

Usually, most of the toddlers participate in cleanup time. A child who has just moved up from the nursery may just stand and watch. Later, she will mimic the behavior of the other children and begin to help by carrying a book to the bookshelf. Victory! But sometimes a child who has worn himself out with vigorous play becomes frustrated with this routine and doesn't want to, or truly cannot, participate. Teachers must be discerning about requiring very young children's participation.

It is futile and unkind to try to force a toddler to put away his toys alone. It is most often just too much for him now. Helping an adult put them away is a more reasonable expectation, except for times when he's clearly just too tired. The capacity for this work is learned over time. Pulling out toys is a natural behavior for the toddler. If he puts away even a few toys, this is evidence of significant growth and deserves a little word of praise. Next year, he'll be able to do more—but right now, he has other work to do.

Toddlers' work

Children have their own work at every stage of development. A child's play is very important work, and he really can't effectively move ahead to the next stage of development until he has completed the job of the present stage. It's a mistake to attempt to push this natural progression along. Doing so will only frustrate the child, his parents, and other grown-up friends. We (usually) must crawl before we can walk.

> CHILDREN HAVE THEIR OWN WORK AT EVERY STAGE OF DEVELOPMENT.

Toddlers and language

During the second year of life, toddlers may begin to acquire some words, but their ability to use language effectively is very limited. This, coupled with the other important and continuing learning challenges during this period, can at times spark frustration in the child. Toddlers are quite capable of experiencing a whole range of emotions, from sadness and fear to joy, excitement, and anger; but they don't typically have enough language to verbally express what they are feeling. This can be pretty overwhelming sometimes, and they may respond to this frustration in some pretty dramatic ways. They need a calm, matter-of-fact response to these behaviors, which reassures them that a bigger, loving person is in control of the things that overwhelm them. This requires much understanding and patience from the adults who care for toddlers.

Toddlers' daily schedules

Toddlers need a reliable schedule in the same way the infants do. All preschoolers thrive on knowing when certain events will occur, including group time, morning snack, outside time, music, lunch, story time, and naptime. When the day is structured for them in simple and understandable terms, they gain a sense of control and reassurance. While the schedule is always very flexible, certain things should happen the way toddlers expect them to. There is much security in this for the child. He learns that his needs are important and someone cares about this and has planned good things for him.

Toddlers and Walking

Toddlers must learn to walk better, and this is a big job. It usually involves a lot of falling. Fortunately, diapers generally do a good job of cushioning many falls. But sometimes these little folks fall and get a "booboo." When this hurts, there are a lot of tears. Other times, it's just discouraging for the little guy who is trying so hard to do this right, and that can bring tears, too. It's not easy to be a toddler. They need a lot of hugs and encouragement from their big friends.

Toddlers and Power

You'll notice that the children in this room seem to move things around a lot. This is partially because of their short attention spans, as we discussed previously. Sometimes, though, it's all about power.

> IT'S NOT EASY TO BE A TODDLER. THEY NEED LOTS OF HUGS AND ENCOURAGEMENT FROM THEIR BIG FRIENDS.

The toddler is moving beyond the complete helplessness of infancy into a brave new world of competency, and on some level he understands this. He has learned, long ago, to turn over when he feels like it. He is able to clap his hands together. He can drink from his sippy cup without help. He enjoys picking up his peas and placing them in his own mouth. He can make many loud sounds and has learned to use some words. And he can walk!

The toddler has learned some other important things that are truly remarkable. For example, he knows that he and his mother are separate from each other. He has also learned that when Mommy and Daddy leave in the morning, they are not gone forever. They come back. These are big concepts that form part of the foundation for the capacity to reason. He has also learned that when he drops his bottle on the floor, a big person will pick it up for him. To think that this young child, in such a brief time, has begun to understand something about the concept of cause and effect is wonderful—even amazing.

I believe that toddlers move objects from here to there with such purpose because in doing so they recognize their own power to exercise influence and control over their world. And this is naturally very important to them. They decide that the teddy bear is going to sit on the window seat, so they pick him up, carry him across the room, and place him right there. And heaven help the parent or teacher or other toddler friend who gets in the way! Each time the toddler does something like this, he gains an increased sense of courage, self-esteem, and confidence, which is very healthy and an important foundation for what comes next.

THE TERRIFIC TWOS

The two-year-olds' class is one of the most exciting areas of the center. In this room are people in the midst of an important and challenging period of development. Just as younger toddlers are beginning to understand that they can have some influence and control over their environment, the twos, often referred to as "older toddlers," are aware of this on a much deeper level.

Toddlers and teenagers

One minute the two-year-old is tired of being a baby and feels ready to be a big girl. Next, she feels threatened by what being a big girl requires of her and she misses the simplicity of being a baby. This is really hard. Life at this stage of development is similar in many ways to what teenagers are experiencing as they struggle to leave childhood, while not yet ready to cope with the responsibilities of adulthood. Both periods of growth can be quite volatile.

Caregivers who have a vision of this "big picture" for twos will have a wonderful time with their little friends. They will not be threatened by occasional outbursts of anger or by the typical tantrums. Teachers learn to ignore much of this. You may notice a caregiver walking around a child who is screaming and thrashing about on the floor. There's no need to intervene unless that child is about to hurt herself or someone else. Instead, the teacher moves to engage other children who are staring at this spectacle with some other particularly interesting activity. The tantruming child soon recognizes this behavior is becoming tiresome, since the pressure of emotions has been released and she no longer has an audience.

Twos need freedom to try new things

The two-year-old classroom is set up in a similar way to the toddler class. This space provides plenty of room for moving around, because twos need this. They have lots and lots of energy.

Children this age are very curious to understand more about how the world works. They need freedom to try—and to fail at—many new things. They need encouragement when they do fail, not criticism. The child who is criticized for every mistake may soon learn to avoid trying new things. And twos need to make many choices for themselves so they can begin to learn what works and what doesn't in a wide variety of competencies.

> THEY NEED FREEDOM TO TRY— AND TO FAIL.

The beginnings of social interaction

True social interaction, however rudimentary, begins in the two-year-old class. Each child will have some wonderful and exciting successes as she becomes more interested in other children and begins to make friends. Each will also experience some setbacks. The child learns that when I share my toys, my friend is happy and we have fun. When I don't share, my friend gets upset or angry at me. And if I hit my friend because he said bad things, he may not want to play with me for (what seems like) a long time. Even if I'm sorry, he may hit me back. Although she's beginning to understand these simple principles, it is often hard at times for a two-year-old to share toys or people.

Cleanup time with twos

The two-year-old can be very cooperative with the teacher when it's time to put toys away. She enjoys the structure of the daily schedule, which includes being a helper at cleanup time. On most days, she thrives on the order and sense of accomplishment this brings. She may instruct others that they aren't doing it right. And her newfound confidence about how things are supposed to work can get her into trouble with her friends.

Two-year-olds and language

While twos are beginning to use short sentences, most still have very limited language skills. This can add to the frustrations they experience every day. Caregivers learn to really listen and soon understand the individual child's language much better than a casual observer can.

The diversity of the language development rate, as well as other areas of development in typically developing two-year-olds, can be quite broad. For example, one day when I walked into the young twos class at Creative Learning Center, a teacher was sitting on the floor with a small group showing them a series of pictures. Each page depicted one simply designed object. When asked what a given object was, the children would respond enthusiastically, "A bunny!" or "It's a fire truck." When she presented one particular picture, however, no one in the group could figure out what it was. A newly enrolled child, whose parents' work had required the family to travel extensively, happened by. Overhearing the question, he responded by saying, "That's a flamingo. We saw those when we were in Spain." The teacher was amazed, since she was just looking for the word *bird*.

That child's language development was obviously way ahead of the game. But his development in other areas was pretty typical. It's not unusual, though, for the child who is advanced in a given area to be a little behind the rest of the group in one or more other areas. The variations in children's development do not necessarily indicate that one child is more intelligent than another or will ultimately possess greater athleticism, for example. And comparing their rates of growth is not valuable, although I've seen people do this.

> WE SHOULD NEVER UNDERESTIMATE THE CHALLENGE, VALUE, AND SIGNIFICANCE OF SIMPLE FIRST STEPS IN ANY AREA OF LEARNING.

Respect for individual development

The truth is, young children can be taught to do tricks, just as a pet can. Sometimes adults teach things so they can "show off" their child to friends or family. But to me, when parents or teachers focus on performance for performance's sake, it seems to be fundamentally disrespectful of who children are and of the awesome capacity for learning that has been built into each of them. They're all just different, each with his or her own developmental timetable in every area in which young children grow and learn. What we truly understand about the way little children acquire knowledge is quite limited. Remember, a good child development program recognizes and values this natural process and avoids tampering with it too much, allowing each child to progress as individual interests dictate.

TWO-YEAR-OLDS AND CREATIVE EXPRESSION

Children this age are able to grasp large crayons and make marks on a paper. This is the beginning of art expression. It's important for adults to avoid critiquing this work with remarks like, "This looks like a flower," when the child only intended to watch color flow out from the crayon or the paintbrush onto the paper. Instead, a comment such as, "I like the way you used that blue color" would be a much more encouraging statement. Holding and manipulating the crayon or brush is a big accomplishment. Adults should not underestimate the challenge, value, and significance of simple first steps in any area of learning.

LEARNING NEW CONCEPTS AND NAMES FOR THINGS

Twos are learning about color by recognizing and naming primary colors first, then purple, orange, and so on. They are beginning to identify and discuss circles, squares, and triangles, and learning about other shapes as well. Often children are taught at home to count up to ten—great fun for proud parents and grandparents. But when children begin to show real interest in numerical concepts, they can also understand what one of something really means, or how to bring three books from the bookshelf to the teacher.

Teachers use a variety of means to help children understand the differences between high and low, up and down, in and out, over and under. And they often sit at the table with their children as they work with equipment and materials that help develop visual perception and discrimination, eye-hand coordination, and fine motor skills.

MUSIC

Twos love music time, where they learn songs such as "The Wheels on the Bus Go Round and Round." Singing with their teacher and friends is fun and helps the child learn the joy of music and of cooperating with friends. A two-year-old can memorize a surprising number of songs. Twos also love to dance. Music in the environment, including a variety of child-friendly and classical music, should be a regular part of the two-year-old classroom experience.

Developing attention spans

Twos are able to pay attention as their teacher reads a brief story or asks children one at a time which is their favorite animal. Attention spans and listening skills are being stretched.

The importance of pretending

Twos enjoy pretending and dressing up in the home center. Their dramatic play can be very interesting to observe as they pretend to be Mommy or Daddy, baby brother, or teacher. In this type of play, children are beginning to understand more about grown-up life. They're learning about the give-and-take of social interaction in yet another way. "Make-believe" can afford a kinder, gentler, more objective experience at times than first-hand social involvement with two-year-old friends.

Toilet training

Toilet training is an important component of the day in the twos' class. There will be a restroom adjoining the class, set aside just for them, to facilitate potty training. A changing station will also be available for those who aren't yet ready for the potty. Twos are proud of themselves and their friends who are learning to use the potty. And sometimes they discuss this among themselves. There can develop a very subtle kind of peer pressure to use the potty—not necessarily a bad thing at this stage.

> REGULAR COMMUNICATION BETWEEN PARENTS AND TEACHERS IS CRITICAL.

Consistency in expectations and approach to toilet training through regular communication between parents and teachers is critical to success. It's important to remember that all children learn to use the toilet, just as they learn to feed themselves and tie their shoes. We don't need to be overly concerned about the timing, except that a child enrolling into a new center should not be expected to begin toilet training until she is settled into the new environment.

> BALANCED EXPECTATIONS ARE IMPORTANT HERE.

When parents and staff are reasonably relaxed about the process, children usually become competent in using the potty some time while they are a two- or young three-year-old. They begin to notice that using the potty takes a good bit less time than a diaper change, which can become very motivating. Adults' anxiety can actually delay the process. Balanced expectations are important here, since pushing a child ahead in toilet training in an attempt to meet some arbitrary deadline is not wise. On the other hand, parents who think it's okay for their typically developing three-and-a-half to four-year-old to be in diapers are not thinking this through. A child in that position can face a lot of very negative peer pressure, which could harm her social development and self-esteem.

Activity centers for twos

The activity centers in the twos' class will be more elaborate than in the toddler room. Book corners will have more available books, and books will be rotated regularly. Home centers have all kinds of dress-up clothes and accessories, including cowboy hats, coats, and construction hard hats for builders. Beautiful shawls, pocketbooks, and hats with feather accents are available for those who want a glamorous touch.

Low shelving offers access to many attractive and appropriately challenging manipulative materials, including many simple puzzles. These items, just as in the infant and toddler room, are age-appropriately designed, recognizing that all children under three, even the twos, are likely to put things into their mouths.

A sand or water table can engage a two-year-old for extended periods. These kinds of sensory experiences are calming and soothe children's emotions. Pouring, sifting, and "measuring" sand and water leads to new discoveries about how these elements work, both separately and when mixed together. This kind of activity also encourages development of fine muscle strength and control.

THE ACTIVITY CENTERS IN THE TWOS' CLASS WILL BE MORE ELABORATE THAN IN THE TODDLER ROOM.

Simple science activities lead children to discover what happens when small cups containing a little water are placed outside the door on a very cold day. Or how a flower can be grown by placing soil into a cup, planting a seed, and watering it. Children check on the progress at the windowsill, watching their plant grow.

OUTDOOR PLAY AND DEVELOPING SKILLS

Outdoors, twos become better at running. They learn to hop. They climb with more agility and can ride on small riding toys. They learn to throw and later catch large balls. They create their own simple games and songs. And they learn to work out some problems with friends. While life with a two-year-old can present some unique challenges to parents and teachers, watching this child learn and mature so much in such a brief period offers the interested, compassionate observer unique rewards as well.

THE PRESCHOOL CLASSROOM

Children between the ages of thirty-six months and five years old have become able explorers. Prior to being promoted into the center's preschool program, they have discovered many things on their own and through the leadership and examples of both friends and teachers, and they are eager to see what comes next. You will notice dramatic developmental changes during this period.

Preschool friends

Preschoolers in this age range are very interested in the other children in their group. They enjoy having friends and are learning how to behave in friendly ways with their classmates. They've begun to understand that cooperating with friends is an important part of life, and they recognize that figuring out how to get along provides practical benefits.

These children can be quite sensitive to the needs of a friend who is having a hard day, and their efforts to reach out to this friend can be very sweet and selfless. Yet, I have frequently seen these same children's demeanor change dramatically the moment Mom or Dad arrives, as they assume behaviors reminiscent of their younger days.

Preschoolers can also experience social challenges in this period of growth, and this occasionally results in verbal and sometimes physical conflict. Typically such conflicts are only brief bumps in the road. Sometimes, though, a child may repeatedly clash with one or two specific peers. The desire to resolve such a problem can be pretty intense for these children, and they sometimes dig themselves into a deeper hole. Teachers redirect these children to other interesting activities, thus providing a "cooling off" period. It's not unusual for the children who have had the most difficulty getting along to ultimately become "best buddies".

Communication skills

Preschool children's vocabulary develops rapidly. Between the ages of three and five years old, children become capable of very effective verbal expression. They are interested in new words and enjoy making up their own words and being silly with language. They love rhymes and new songs. And they can be very good at telling jokes or at storytelling. I often enjoyed overhearing preschoolers' conversations while wandering through their classrooms. It's truly remarkable how mature their perspectives and their communication skills can sometimes be.

Competitiveness

The preschool child can be very competitive. Being first or best at things may become important to her during this period. She enjoys playing games but can become overly concerned about winning as she learns quickly that this is an important object of certain activities. She may need reminders that just having fun is a valuable part of game-playing, too. Such reminders help relieve some of her pressure to always be the winner.

"I can do it myself"

Preschoolers are becoming better able to dress themselves and often enjoy choosing their clothing for the day. During this period of development, your child's caregiver is probably encouraging children to put their coats and hats on themselves before going outdoors to play. Many parents take the extra time needed at home to allow children to make their own choices, so long as the outfit selected is appropriate for the day's weather. This fosters a healthy sense of self-sufficiency and personal responsibility.

You may notice that when your child reaches this stage, she is also becoming enthusiastic about helping you with certain household chores. This is a great opportunity to build the child's sense of self-worth, as you provide ways for her to participate in tasks such as placing silverware and napkins at the table. She learns that her contribution to family life is really quite important to everyone.

LEARNING RIGHT FROM WRONG

During the preschool years, young children acquire some important moral values, including learning right from wrong. If your child tests boundaries in this area, such as telling a lie, or bringing home a toy from his classroom to keep for himself, it is important that parents and caregivers avoid overreacting. A simple, honest talk that encourages the child to own up to what he did is much more effective. When we model right behaviors for our children, they are much less likely to embrace the wrong ones. It is important to have a direct discussion about right versus wrong choices when children experiment with inappropriate behavior. If we respond to problems in this area appropriately—calmly and firmly, rather than with anger and condemnation—such behavior is much less likely to be repeated.

> PRESCHOOLERS ARE ACQUIRING SOME IMPORTANT MORAL VALUES, INCLUDING LEARNING RIGHT FROM WRONG.

IMAGINATION, FANTASY, AND REALITY

One of the important ways the preschool child uses imagination is in dramatic play. While pretending to be a fireman or a teacher, he will at times become completely immersed in his role. As I observed children engaged in this activity, I often sensed that what they were imagining was very real to them. Some children have an imaginary friend who can be quite real and who can continue "being friends" with the child over a long period of time. The capacity for such vivid imagination can present some problems. Sometimes children can have trouble distinguishing fantasy from reality during the early years.

The "Why?" Question

Young children often ask this important question. It is a big part of their job to learn how life works; therefore, it is important for parents and caregivers to be patient when there seems to be no end to their children's questions, including this one. Taking time to answer the child in simple, accessible terms helps the preschooler understand more about himself, his friends, and the world around him.

Multi-age versus single-age groupings

Some centers group children together with separate classes for three-year-olds, four-year-olds, and pre-kindergarteners. Others choose to group three- to five-year-olds together in the same class. Both approaches can work. The overall physical setup of the classroom in either case is much the same, with equipment and materials that meet specific developmental needs of preschool-aged children.

> BOTH APPROACHES CAN WORK.

The three-year-old whose class consists of only three-year-olds faces fewer types of social challenges, since everyone in the class is close to his own developmental level. This provides a kind of security for certain children. And his teacher has to plan only for threes. But while enjoying these benefits, he misses out on some other good things.

The three-year-old who is integrated into a group of three- to five-year-olds experiences an environment that is more like a very large family. Older children model positive social and other behaviors for the younger children, which can encourage certain kinds of development in the younger group. At the same time, older children learn about patience and compassion as they play and work with younger children who have become their friends. They recognize their younger friends are not yet able to do some of the things they have learned and often help younger children to learn.

Space for group time

The preschool classroom allows space for the whole class to be seated together on the floor for certain types of activities, directed by their teacher. They come together as a group at certain times of the day—for example, for morning circle, where everyone is greeted and they and their teachers talk about today's weather, the topic of the week, and so on. Later, after children have had some time in centers, they may join their teacher as a group for music, singing familiar songs and learning new ones.

Some teachers like to use carpet squares to designate specific seating for the children and avoid the puppy-like activity among preschoolers that sometimes erupts spontaneously. This area is also used for story time and other whole-group activities. Expect to see an open area set aside for such purposes. Children enjoy times like these with their teachers when relaxed and comfortable on the floor, more than they would seated in chairs at the tables. These gatherings foster a sense of belonging within a group, giving classmates a sense of community.

Preschool classroom activity centers

Activity centers in the preschool classroom are critical to the effective developmental program. Teachers add new materials regularly, so children's interest is always keen. The number of children who use a particular center at one time is restricted to maximize this experience for participants. The typically developing preschooler who has ready access to richly structured and equipped activity centers will love coming to school and will sometimes be not quite ready to leave at day's end. This is not because they're not excited to see Mom or Dad. They just want their parent(s) to come into their world and enjoy it with them. Parents are wise to spend a little time this way whenever possible, since this affords insights into your child's day care experience in ways nothing else can.

The Book Corner

Book corners will have a great variety of attractive books that are rotated often. There should be some special books each week, related to that week's theme. These often come from the public library, and teachers can use these borrowed books as an opportunity for teaching our responsibility to take particular care of things that belong to others. There may be large pillows or beanbag chairs on the floor for comfortable reading. The book corner will be separated from more active areas such as the block center. It will be an attractive, calm place that provides plenty of light and perhaps a plant or two. The pre-k class may have a special place in their book corner for the class goldfish.

The Block Center

The block center has plenty of level floor space and a good variety of blocks and accessories, such as cars, trucks, planes, and people figures, for constructing all kinds of things, from single buildings to whole towns. Often children work cooperatively to create, using their imaginations and communication skills to decide how the village they've built is going to work. Teachers are watchful and sensitive to the extra time needed when children decide on their own to engage in an elaborate project.

> PRETENDING ENABLES THE CHILD TO LEARN SOME THINGS ABOUT BEING AN ADULT.

The Art Center

The art center will be filled with materials that facilitate the young child's free expression of artistic beauty. Children will have regular access to paints, brushes, and small easels. There are safety scissors and papers of every variety and color. Child-safe paste and glue is available for making collages, as is everything from cotton balls to sequins to feathers for this purpose. Pipe cleaners, home-made play dough and modeling clays make wonderful sculptures. Big pencils and other colored pencils are accessible along with plain white paper for drawing. And adults express genuine interest in the artwork created by each child. The minimal time it takes to listen to the child who is showing a parent or teacher his artwork for that day is a big investment into his confidence and healthy self-esteem.

The Home (Dramatic Play) Center

The home center will be outfitted for all kinds of dramatic play. It will provide lots of dress-up clothes and hats, since it is the base of operations for everybody from doctors to firemen to teachers to royalty. After all, everyone starts and ends their day at home. At times, teachers extend this center's use to include a store with items "for sale," or set up the area as a theater where actors put on a show. Sometimes dolls will be part of the play and will be fed, or read or sung to, or will need time out to think about things. Sometimes people will do chores they see their parents do at home, such as cooking, putting away groceries, or sweeping the floor. Others give speeches, and their friends must sit and listen. The audience knows that later they'll have a chance to tell everyone what will happen next. Child-safe mirrors are important here so children can see how grown up they look in their pretending clothes. The work of pretending is very important to young children, because through this play they discover some things about what it means to be an adult woman or man.

Manipulative Materials

The manipulative materials shelf will be close to tables. Children often call these pieces of equipment their "tabletop toys." This equipment is designed to support children's cognitive development. It also encourages visual perception and fine motor skills development. Use of these materials involves quiet play that encourages children to focus on the problem at hand. When this area is properly structured, it will be very appealing to children. They will return here again and again, enjoying these fun activities while all kinds of pre-academic readiness skills are being strengthened.

The Computer Center

Many preschool classrooms have computer centers where children learn some basic skills with games and activities designed just for them. These centers are very popular, and as in all other centers, we learn to take turns. The computer center may be next to an audio center, where children listen to music or stories through headphones.

Sensory Tables

Sensory tables are often set up in or near the art area where cleanup is easy. Plastic bins are filled with a variety of things such as water, sand, or mud. Most preschool children enjoy the soothing effect of pouring, sifting, and measuring various materials.

The Science Center

The science center may include a terrarium or an aquarium with a variety of fish. Children take turns watering plants or feeding the fish each day, with their teacher's supervision. Chairs are provided for the child who wants to sit quietly and watch the fish for a while, which is a very calming experience.

The Quiet Corner

Often a small area is set aside for individual quiet time somewhere in the room, recognizing that sometimes a child may wish to be alone, away from all the action. This area is not used for required "time-outs." Preschool classrooms are busy places, and a child may occasionally need some time by himself with his own thoughts.

> A CHILD MAY SOMETIMES NEED TIME ALONE WITH HIS OWN THOUGHTS.

Theme-Related Centers and Activities

In addition to the centers previously described, teachers often set up special theme-related activities at tables where children take turns participating. For example, a class studying restaurants may participate with their teacher and the center's cook in some carefully supervised cooking activities that week.

Often teachers plan outdoor activities related to the topic of the week. For example, during "Fall Week," children might gather colored leaves, pinecones, or acorns from the playground, bringing them into class to make beautiful lunch table centerpieces.

10

THE PEOPLE

We were fortunate to have employed numerous degreed teachers who worked in our center for several years before going on into a public or private elementary school. I was always on the lookout for potential staff members who had credentials in early childhood education, child development, or a related field. Rosemary had just completed her bachelor's degree and told me of her plans to pursue a graduate degree in another year. For now, she wanted to gain preschool classroom experience as a lead teacher, and we needed a lead teacher.

Rosemary was very knowledgeable. And she was friendly and outgoing. As we toured our center, she obviously enjoyed meeting our staff, observing the activity in each of their classrooms, and she seemed to approve of what she saw. But she never really engaged with any of the children. She actually stiffened a bit when our pre-k class came in from their playground on that hot, dusty August morning. They were all talking at once, needing to get their dirty little hands and faces washed up for lunch. I noticed that Rosemary took a step back as the exuberant throng entered the classroom, and her manner told me this wasn't just because she needed to guard her interview attire.

Why did I choose not to hire Rosemary? Because after years of interviewing potential staff members, I had developed a sense of which applicants were more likely to have "staying power" in day care. Her demeanor communicated some reservations about work with preschoolers. I was concerned that Rosemary's interest in our children had more to do with her desire to experiment with how educational theory plays out in practice than with wanting to get to know and be involved with the individual children in our program. We needed a lead teacher for whom the latter motivation was at least as important as the former.

YOU WILL MEET A LOT OF NEW PEOPLE ON YOUR TOUR. You may be terrific with names, but if you're not, don't worry. What you need to learn right now is not the names of people, but how they relate with others, particularly with children, and some indication about their character. These are the individuals who will have so much influence on your child's life if you choose to enroll, so you need to watch for some signs. I'll share some of these with you in this chapter.

THE DIRECTOR

The director of the child care center or family day home you choose is the person who will have the greatest impact on the overall effectiveness of the program over time. Whether the program works well or poorly will be in large measure a result of this person's leadership. Most of the people in director positions will be women.

WELCOMING YOU

What is your impression when you first meet her? Does she make you feel welcome and try to put you at ease? Does she overwhelm you with a flurry of questions, or does she talk for a while, sharing some things about the program, and allowing you to get used to her personality and to determine whether she seems easy to be around? In other words, does she give you time to "size her up"?

Do you begin to gain a sense of what is important to her? Do you feel that she is someone you can talk to, someone who really cares about your needs? Does she ask about what your child enjoys and whether he has had the opportunity to be with other adults and children, and how he felt about that? Is she interested in why you are seeking child care and in knowing what kind of work you do? A good director will respect the fact that ultimately you are interviewing her, not the other way around.

> YOU NEED SOME INDICATION OF STAFF MEMBERS' CHARACTER.

Helping to bring out the best in people

If a child development program is to be effective, the director must be a good facilitator of human relationships. Most of the real benefits a good program offers to children are relationship-driven; therefore, the director serves as a kind of "air traffic controller" to help people avoid bumping into one another. This requires her to model kindness and patience and self-control for staff members and children. She will be prepared to intervene when needed to help people resolve the conflicts that are a normal part of life.

She must understand how to work effectively with staff who are rarely adequately recognized for the value they bring to people's lives. Yet, if the program is to meet the real needs of children, each staff member must function at a very high level every day—in a job that is both physically and emotionally challenging and does not pay very well. The director must possess leadership qualities that bring out the best in each staff member and that foster mutual respect among caregivers and auxiliary staff for the sake of the children in their care and everyone else involved.

The director also ensures that staff members can agree on important child development goals, including issues like discipline and values teaching. This protects children from the confusion they would otherwise suffer when promoting from one class to the next.

What if your three-year-old is taught that he doesn't need to wash the paint out of his paintbrush when he's through with it, or put away the library's special book on the shelf where borrowed books are kept? A teacher who routinely does things for children that they are capable of doing for themselves may really believe this is best for them—she may think young children should be protected from unpleasant tasks. Or she may be taking the easy way out, because doing these chores herself is easier and faster than teaching responsibility. Such a teacher would be at odds with most preschool teachers, who recognize that performing routine chores fosters maturity.

> THE DIRECTOR IS A KIND OF "AIR TRAFFIC CONTROLLER".

If teachers in the same center disagree on such basic things, how do children know which of their grown-up friends is right about taking care of paintbrushes or library books? Whose guidance is important—and whose can they disregard? Creating the right overall environment for young children requires unanimity among the staff.

MERCY MIXED WITH ORGANIZATION

The individual who effectively manages a large child care center or who runs a wonderful family day home must be a person of mercy—inclined toward compassion, kindness and understanding. She will have the heart of a servant. Her whole orientation will be toward meeting people's needs, and this is the place from which her joy and satisfaction derive. Her fulfillment will not come from being the one in charge, exercising power over everyone and everything. Her fulfillment will be in seeing people's real needs being met, including those of children and parents, and certainly those of her staff.

The director will possess strong organizational skills. The volume and diversity of issues she manages every day requires this. Without this capacity, she would quickly become overwhelmed by the intensity of ever-present needs, and things would quickly fall off track.

The director's relationship with children and parents

The director will be seeking to know and understand you and your child, and to know how she can genuinely reassure both of you about your new way of life. If you enroll in her program, she will be watching to see how your child is adjusting, not just on the first day or two, but ongoing over a period of weeks and months. And she will provide extra staff when possible so your child's primary caregiver will have more one-on-one time with him, making adjustment to day care easier.

She will also be watching you to know where you are in this transition, as you come to know and trust her and the caregivers and staff who work in the center.

Protecting Your Parental Rights

The effective director will let you know you are welcome to stop in at any time, unannounced, to assure yourself that everything is all right. She will provide ways for you to observe your child without him knowing you are there, such as through two-way mirrors. (This is to protect him from a second separation experience, which would confuse him and make his adjustment more difficult.)

This director will encourage you to call anytime to check on your child's day. In our program, parents were normally able to reach caregivers in the classroom or on the playground whenever they called. We set these impromptu communications between parents and caregivers as a priority and structured things accordingly. Having some supplemental staff makes it possible for a primary caregiver to spend a little longer with you when she returns your call, in the event she can't speak immediately.

Teaching Values Together

Your values for your child are important to a wise director. She is aware that if the values taught by the program are in conflict with your own, your child will be placed in an untenable position. It is not fair for a young child to try to discern right from wrong when his teacher tells him to be kind to the other children and that hitting is not allowed, while his parent has taught him to stand up for himself aggressively, resulting in fighting at every turn. Regardless of their religious backgrounds, most parents are happy for their child to learn things like respect for others, personal responsibility, kindness, and self-control. You and the director should address the kinds of values the school tries to instill in children, assuring one another of mutual support so you both know you're on the same track in this important area.

Knowing Your Child and His Individual Needs

The director knows the children in each class—not only their names, but also a lot about their temperament, their likes and dislikes, whether they have any food or other allergies, and so on. She understands how her program is affecting each child and whether adjustments should be made to accommodate a particular need. The children know her as one of their grown-up friends.

Over time, she will, for example, know if your child is having problems with another child or is not eating well at lunchtime. And she will not hide things from you. She will want you to know everything about your child's life in day care because she understands your need and right to be kept informed.

She looks forward to meeting with you to help resolve a problem or concern. She is willing to work diligently to meet any need you bring to her attention. At the same time, she'll be candid about any limitations in her ability to comply with a particular request.

Encouraging Parental Involvement

A good director recognizes the benefit of parental participation and input in the program. She offers opportunities for parents to become involved through a Parent Advisory Board. The parents' perspectives on the day-to-day life of the center are very valuable, because they often offer suggestions that improve the effectiveness of the center's service to them and their children. And many parents enjoy helping with special events and projects throughout the year.

> SHE WILL HAVE THE HEART OF A SERVANT — HER FULFILLMENT IS IN SEEING PEOPLE'S REAL NEEDS BEING MET.

The thoughtful director finds ways to communicate with parents individually, as well as with the parent group as a whole. Families benefit by getting to better know the staff and others in the parent group. Lots of photos of children at work and play indicate that this director wants you to understand your child's life in preschool.

The director may provide comfortable outdoor seating near the playground, encouraging parents to linger and visit together from time to time in the late afternoons. Newsletters, single-classroom parties, and whole-center festivals and picnics are some other ways your center's director may foster free-flowing communication and parental involvement. An effective director recognizes that a community of caring adult friends is one of the finest things she has to offer the children.

Protecting Everyone's Interests

Finally, this individual understands her responsibility to all of the children, parents, and staff in the program and will expect you to abide by center policies while your child is enrolled. If you do not, you will hear from her. Your director has much to protect and will expect every parent to pay tuition and fees and to pick up their child on time. She recognizes what her role in the families' lives is and what it is not. She will not be the family's banker, lending money from her limited budget so parents can pay late. Nor will she fail to enforce policies guarding against her and her staff from having to play babysitter if parents are late picking up their children. It is unrealistic to expect to enroll in a strong program, enjoying all the benefits this brings for the child and the family, and then be casual about holding up your end of the bargain. Allowing families to ignore center policies puts everyone's positions in jeopardy, and a good director will not take such risks.

> PARENTS MUST NOT BE CASUAL ABOUT HOLDING UP THEIR END OF THE BARGAIN.

THE DIRECTOR'S RELATIONSHIP WITH STAFF

A good director has a strong orientation toward meeting the caregivers' needs. The day-to-day work of caregivers is where the program succeeds or fails. Remaining available to staff throughout the day and reaching out to them regularly ensures she meets their needs for supplies, materials, or extra help. She "manages by wandering around"[1] in the center, casually visiting with parents, staff, and children, and always watching for unmet needs or any area requiring her intervention.

Providing Appropriate Equipment, Materials, and Training

Child care center staff members need certain resources in order to be effective in their work. The director monitors various needs indoors and out to be sure that equipment and materials are adequately maintained and supplied.

All staff members participate in ongoing professional training, which is provided at the program's expense. This creative, informative training encourages caregivers to continue moving toward more and more effective service for children. Times set aside for training also allow staff members time together when children aren't present—this fellowship renews staff members' enthusiasm for their work. The director makes sure that state regulatory requirements are met or exceeded in the area of continuing professional education.

Providing the Right Structure

However gifted, well-trained, and devoted to children an individual may be, no caregiver can remain effective for long if she's responsible for too many children. Nor can she manage her class well if the room is too small or if she doesn't have sufficient equipment and materials. Such problems for caregivers also present some serious problems for children.

Each state has its own requirements for acceptable adult-to-child ratios and typically designates a certain amount of floor space for each child in a classroom. These two numbers are among the most significant factors affecting the costs of any child development program. For the sake of the children, often the director or board of directors will do more than what the law requires, even though it is costly.

If a director chooses to ignore the staff's needs in how the program is structured, she will eventually lose them. Be sure to ask how long staff members have been employed in the programs you are considering. It is a very good sign if a program has a history of employment longevity with many staff members. If staff turnover is excessive, this may indicate a structural problem that could preclude the calm, relaxed environment your child needs.

Protecting Process through Communication

The director cultivates relationships with staff members because she genuinely respects and appreciates them and their work. While caregivers know she is on their side, they also know she is the one in charge, faithfully enforcing center policies for the protection of everyone. A comfortable relationship between caregivers and director facilitates ready and free communication when problems arise. The director needs to know how things are going for everyone so she can effectively intervene if any trouble develops.

Staff job descriptions and personnel policies are clear about each individual's responsibilities. These are fair, understandable, and reasonable, and they establish the foundation for how everyone will work with one another. Staff members must accept their responsibility to abide by these rules before they are employed. Disregard of center policies by its personnel can put children at risk and is therefore not tolerated.

> EXCESSIVE STAFF TURNOVER MAY INDICATE A STRUCTURAL PROBLEM THAT COULD PRECLUDE THE CALM, RELAXED ENVIRONMENT YOUR CHILD NEEDS.

Confronting Threats to Joy

The effective director greatly encourages her staff members to work hard to protect their relationships and the joy they have in their work. Gossip and strife among caregivers and center staff can be deadly for any child care program. So the director establishes clear expectations about this offense and is willing to take strong action, including dismissal, to protect the children from the insidious fallout of such misery.

THE CAREGIVERS

The majority of people working in the child development field are women. However, as the demand for child care services in our country has risen, the awareness of the significance of this work in its influence on the young child has also grown. Increasingly more men are now working in this field. Male caregivers who have the right combination of knowledge and skill suitable for day care can be a big benefit to children, many of whom grow up in homes with a single mother. Just as grade school children do, preschool children also need strong, positive male role models.

Staff qualifications

The women and men who effectively work with young children over time have a particular orientation of the heart. Ideally, they will possess some formal education in the field of child development and/or early childhood education, either an associate's or bachelor's degree. The information and perspectives gained from education specific to this work is of tremendous value. However, possessing knowledge about how things should work for the young child is not a guarantee that the individual will actually be able to provide and maintain such an environment. Something more is needed.

Often when I interviewed prospective staff members and asked the applicant why she wanted to work with young children, I would hear at some point, "I want to work in day care because I just love children." This is always good to hear, but I came to understand that I couldn't take this statement at face value. Sometimes when people say this, they really mean they have been around a child or children for whom they have a personal affection. An inexperienced caregiver, even one who has studied child development, may think the happy experiences they have had with certain children is indicative of what it will be like to work among young children all day, five days a week. Mere affection is not sufficient to maintain the demanding standards required for effective work with children. Affections come and go. Something more is needed.

It's important for the program director to spend time personally interviewing the applicants who are being seriously considered as caregivers. There's a lot to be learned through just talking together. And it is preferable to find an individual whose staying power has been proven through previous experience in day care. A good reference from that program's director as well as the individual's coworkers there can be very helpful.

Licensing regulations in Tennessee require that any person who works in a child care center or family day home must undergo a background check, which includes fingerprinting, by the Tennessee Bureau of Investigation. This is to ensure that person has no criminal background that could place a child at risk. Additionally, research must be done to ensure the legitimacy of personal character references and of work history. Caregivers must prove that they are in good health through a physician's health exam and certification.

The good candidate understands and appreciates why the center establishes policies, including personnel policies, for the protection of everyone. She will faithfully support these reasonable policies with integrity. Still, something more is needed.

I believe there are three personal characteristics a caregiver must have to work effectively in the best interest of young children over time.

Saying she loves children isn't enough...Does she like them?

First, this person must have an intuitive understanding of young children and why they do the things they do. And she must like them and the things they do. Anyone can say, "I love children." That's easy. But sometimes the person making this statement is merely indicating her personal affection for her idea of who young children are. Truly liking children comes when the caregiver has taken time to observe them more closely, coming to understand, appreciate, and respect why they do what they do. This deeper understanding enables her to continue giving to the child when she personally is having a hard day. This individual can commit herself to what is best for each child unconditionally while the child is under her care and supervision.

The good caregiver will enjoy what children do and the choices they make for themselves, including those choices that could drive a reasonable, sane person to distraction. She will actually like the developmental processes inherent in the young child's life.

In a practical sense, this means that when the toddler deliberately pours his milk into his plate at lunchtime, the caregiver will not take personal offense. It's possible for a caregiver to respond to this situation with a textbook-perfect response while actually being quite frustrated with this little boy within her heart. At times, even the best caregivers will experience frustration with the children they serve, just as parents will, because we are all human. However, this will not be her typical response to situations such as this one.

> SHE WILL ACTUALLY LIKE THE DEVELOPMENTAL PROCESSES INHERENT IN THE YOUNG CHILD'S LIFE.

The effective caregiver will recognize that the child probably did not do this to make her day more difficult. Rather, he's likely just interested in learning what liquid can do. Or he may be exploring cause and effect, to see what might happen. He could be well served to first help clean up, and at some point later that day, perhaps after naptime is over, be offered some extra time at the water play table. The caregiver who overreacts to an incident like this actually elicits more of this behavior from the child, which then can become motivated by a contest of wills rather than the child's initial interest—the toddler version of scientific exploration.

A TEACHABLE SPIRIT

Second, the excellent caregiver is herself a teachable person. The truth is we can all learn from one another. Everyone has gifts and experiences unique to them and instructive to others. All of us have the capacity to continue to learn and grow throughout life. It's important to find preschool teachers and caregivers who have the kind of joy in learning that we see in the young child.

It is wonderful to find folks, including those with years of experience in the field, who recognize that there is always more for them to learn. The person who has adequate self-confidence, personal flexibility, and humility to realize that even a brand-new caregiver might come up with something great that she never thought of brings a joyful expectancy to her work. This approach facilitates respectful relationships among staff members. And this person doesn't miss the things each child can teach his adult friends.

Part of the work of a good child development program is the ongoing professional training and development of its staff. Teachers will be involved in workshops and seminars, both on-site and off-site, at various times throughout each year. And the teachable person won't resent this expenditure of her time. In addition to continuing to learn more about how best to support developmental processes in children, staff will be trained and certified in first aid and infant/child CPR.

> THE EXCELLENT CAREGIVER IS HERSELF A TEACHABLE PERSON.

THE HEART OF A SERVANT

Having a servant's heart is the third quality I believe necessary for caregivers to deliver to children what they need most from them.

Children can be very discerning. They recognize when an adult is genuinely interested in them versus a feigned pretense of interest. A child's personal self-concept is formed in relation to significant persons, especially the closest adults in their lives. Every child needs to have healthy self-esteem. So the true heart of the effective caregiver will be one of joyful service. She will take pleasure in serving children.

In my own spiritual life, my personal example for servanthood is Jesus Christ. It is my personal belief that He is the one who said, "Let there be light."[2] And there was light. Yet, when He came to earth as a man, it was clear that He came for the purpose of serving, not to be served. The One who possessed the greatest power poured Himself out for me, one of the powerless. What a great example for those who work with children!

People who have a servant's heart deeply recognize the truth of the words, "It is more blessed to give than to receive."[3] They get that. And the fact that they get that impacts the words they say and actions they take with children. It is their heartfelt joy to give of themselves into the life of a little child, including times when no one else sees or notices. For very little financial reward and virtually no societal recognition, day after day they consistently pour out their lives on behalf of young children, offering the kind of love and encouragement for which no amount of money could ever adequately compensate them. They don't do it because it's an easy job, because it is not easy. They don't do it in an effort to force their personal faith on anyone, because that is not their place. They do it purely for the joy of serving. When a director finds someone like that, she has found gold.

Look at the faces

As you make your way through the classrooms, from the nursery to pre-k, observe the manner in which the caregivers interact with children. Look at their faces. Do they enjoy the children and their work? Do they seem relaxed and comfortable in the environment? Do they handle tough situations positively and with patience? Do you see mutually respecting interactions between staff members, as well with any parents who may be present? If the center you're visiting is large, you may come upon a caregiver who is not having her best day. Do the others around her seem to be taking up a little of her slack? If you recognize that the great majority of the staff members in this program seem to feel content and at home here, in the midst of what is periodically quite busy, demanding work, you should seriously consider this center.

THE CHILDREN

The other children enrolled in the center you choose will be an important part of your child's life at day care. Observing them closely as you are touring this program will give important indications about how the program will affect your child.

At home in the environment

Do the children seem relaxed and at home in this environment? Are they freely engaged in work or play, actively involved with things that interest them? Do they seem to have a kind of proprietary attitude toward their classroom—do you get the sense that the children here feel that this room and the things in it belong to them?

If you are present in a preschool classroom while a whole-group activity is taking place, do most of the children join the others for group time with positive expectations? Do most of them seem to be enjoying the activity? Does the teacher seem to be managing the group effectively, skillfully juggling the needs of the various children who want to talk at the same time? And does she seem to know where she is going with the subject matter she is covering, indicating that she has prepared well for this activity? Does the children's interest level reflect that this is so?

When group time is over and children move to the activities centers, does this transition occur in a reasonably orderly manner? Do the children cooperate with each other as they share spaces and equipment? If there are conflicts, how are these resolved? Are children given some opportunity to attempt resolution on their own?

Do you see lots of children's artwork displayed at their own eye level so they can examine it closely when they wish? Does their art show evidence of teachers who encourage children to express their own feelings and artistic ideas freely, resulting in a wide variety of artworks in the class? Are there any art projects that demonstrate children have worked cooperatively to make this piece?

Rainy days

If there seem to be many conflicts or whining or fussiness among children on the day you tour a program you've consistently heard great things about, is it raining? Or is a storm front moving in? Rainy days can impact children's group behavior in surprising ways. Are teachers sensitive to this with plans for indoor gross motor activities such as dancing or exercise, or brief outside-voices-inside sessions that help children get some of their energy out? Does the center have a gym or a large open room children can use in inclement weather? If not, what is their plan for an extended period of bad weather that prevents children from using their playground?

Special attention

If they want one, do children get a hug from their caregiver for no particular reason? And if a child seems to have a need or is in distress, do you sense that he is confident in his relationship with the teacher? Does he go to her expecting that she 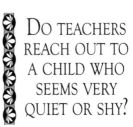 DO TEACHERS REACH OUT TO A CHILD WHO SEEMS VERY QUIET OR SHY?

will listen to and help him? Does he seem to really know and love his teacher?

Do teachers make extra effort to reach out to a child who is very quiet or shy? Do they also reach out to any child who is behaving repeatedly in out-of-bounds behavior, engaging her in interesting one-on-one activities or asking her to be their special helper in some meaningful way that she responds to?

ADMINISTRATIVE AND OTHER STAFF

Ideally, every person employed by the child care center will take their personal job seriously and will work hard to do it well, and they will recognize and enjoy contributing to the center's overall mission. They will be thoughtful people who see the important role they play in facilitating overall goals. When things work this way, they participate in the joy of serving children.

Each person affects everyone else

In our center, the kitchen was adjacent to the primary entrance used by most parents. A counter-height wall separated the kitchen from that primary entrance area; therefore, our cook was the first person many of our parents spoke to in the mornings. We were very fortunate to have several really good cooks who were also cheerful people. The benefits of this to parents and children were obvious, since their friendly greeting in the mornings set the tone for everyone's day. Contrast that atmosphere with the effect of meeting a grumpy, complaining personality first thing each morning. The distress of that could negatively affect each person walking by.

> Parents and families can form friendships that last beyond preschool.

Every person who works in the center has an impact on everyone else. It isn't reasonable to expect that every staff member will be feeling chipper every day of the week—we must allow one another to be human. But it is reasonable to expect that your child's program director will be cognizant of the impact all staff members have on the overall environment for children and will make staffing decisions that include this consideration.

VENDORS AND VISITORS

There are people who come in and out of a day care program every week who provide a variety of commercial services for the center. This can include food service and supplies delivery personnel, as well as lawn care and other utilities maintenance people. Does the center have a camera system that allows staff to see who is coming? Is there a designated staff member who is present with or monitoring these people while they are on campus?

What are the center's policies relative to visitors? A good program will give parent tours regularly. How is this handled? While parents of enrolled children should always have access to the center, visitors who do not have this direct connection with the program should always be accompanied by a staff member.

OTHER PARENTS

Often the parents who enroll their children into a good program stay for several years. Many continue enrollment from the time their child is six weeks old until he graduates from pre-k class and goes on to kindergarten. You'll discover that you have a lot in common with the parents enrolled in the same child development program as you. And in the right atmosphere, parents and families can form friendships that last beyond preschool.

In our program, we often had families who first met each other at our center and developed friendships that brought them and their children together socially outside the center. This is ideal for these parents and their children. Staff members benefit, too, since these relationships inevitably serve to strengthen the overall sense of community in the center.

11

THE SCHEDULES

hen Mrs. Andren walked into my office carrying her toddler on her hip, I could tell she was upset. She got right to the point, telling me that her personal experience with our program since Jeremy started that morning was not living up to what she had been told by her coworkers, or by me. Her fifteen-month-old child's primary caregiver had not been present when she arrived a few minutes before at 5:00 p.m. She complained that she understood that Ms. Martha would be with Jeremy all day, and she didn't know where Martha was or who that person was in his classroom now.

As it happened, Mrs. Andren had not had time to stay to meet Jeremy's afternoon caregiver on her pre-enrollment visits. On the two occasions that she was able to come, she had stopped by very briefly during her own lunch hour. April, the college student who worked with Ms. Martha from 1:30 to 6:00, was in class at the nearby university at that time. While Martha had explained that her work hours were from 7:30 to 4:30 and that Mrs. Andren would find the afternoon staffer supervising Jeremy when she came for him between 5:00 and 5:30 each day, Mrs. Andren had obviously forgotten. There is a lot of new information to assimilate when enrolling into a new center, and as we've said, it's often an emotional time, so it's easy to forget a detail. While April recognized Mrs. Andren from her photograph and checked her personal ID, the recognition was not mutual. Finding her child with someone she hadn't met before, Jeremy's mom was naturally very concerned.

PARENTS NEED AND HAVE THE RIGHT TO BE INFORMED about daily schedules. You should know your caregiver's schedule, including times when she is taking a personal day or is on vacation. On the rare occasion that another staff member swaps work hours with your child's caregiver to meet your caregiver's personal need, for example, for a doctor appointment, you will be informed of this, too. Anytime a substitute teacher takes your caregiver's place, you should be informed and introduced to this person.

It is important that staff members' work schedules are planned to provide for appropriate supervision of children throughout the child care day, and this intricate plan requires that every member of the team is responsible for being at her assigned place during her scheduled work hours. Schedules for children, however, should provide for meeting needs while maintaining plenty of flexibility to accommodate the realities of life with children.

THE DIRECTOR'S SCHEDULE

Full-day child care centers and family day homes typically offer their services over eleven to twelve hours per day. Obviously this is to meet the needs of families whose work schedules differ. Some days the director will be present throughout this period. However, the director is unable to be present on-site each hour the center is open, every day of the week. At times when she is not present, she will remain available to staff by phone. This way she can manage any urgent need or other unusual problem that arises in her absence.

The program's director will often vary her work schedule in order to monitor the effectiveness of the program at different times of the day and week. If the program is open from 7:00 a.m. to 6:00 p.m., she may work from 7:00 to 4:00 one day, or for several days, and from 9:00 to 6:00 over another period. This allows her to observe any structural problems that develop. For example, sometimes the schedules of the parent group shift slightly, causing a need for scheduling adjustments in one or more staff members' work hours.

The director may schedule the assistant director's hours so that this individual will be present from the very beginning of the day, while she may schedule an administrative assistant to be there until closing. This way, on a day when the director works from 9:00 to 5:00, there will be someone present who is "in charge" throughout that day.

THE CAREGIVERS' SCHEDULES

Just like the director, your child's teacher won't be in the center all the time. You will learn her work hours and will know when you'll see her. Several caregivers will be scheduled to help "open" the center. If your child's primary caregiver is one of these and you leave early for work, she'll be present in your child's class to greet you each morning. And she will remain with this group throughout her workday. But if you arrive more than eight or nine hours later to pick up your child, she may have already gone home. In that case, you may find one of the part-time afternoon staff members, an assistant teacher, supervising your child. This person will be assigned to your child's classroom on a routine basis, so you and your

> STAFFING SCHEDULES PROVIDE FOR ADEQUATE SUPERVISION IN EACH CLASS THROUGHOUT THE DAY.

child will get to know her well, too. The consistency of seeing the same teachers each day is very important for your child, and the director will do everything possible to maintain that.

This need for consistency in caregivers will extend to the director's choice for substitute teachers. In a large program, the director is able to keep several substitutes busy. She may hire some "floating subs" who are present on-site and available every day. On days when they're not needed in a particular class, they help teachers with special activities for children. Or they may assist the director in a variety of ways. Sometimes they fill in so a teacher may spend extra time in the Teacher Resource Room, planning for her class. These individuals are invaluable to the program, since all teachers periodically need a vacation week or a day off. Regular substitutes get to know and be known by all the children in the program. They are accustomed to the program's schedules, activities, and management principles and fit right in when needed.

THE CHILDREN'S SCHEDULES

Expect to be kept informed about what your child and her class will be doing throughout each day. The class schedule will be posted so you can refer to it from time to time. Again, this schedule will not be followed rigidly but will serve as an overall guide, allowing for appropriate flexibility.

Teachers who plan appropriately for young children understand the importance of a general consistency in daily schedules. Children feel confident and secure when they know what's coming next. If activities occur in a haphazard or chaotic manner, children don't know what to expect, which can result in tension and distress.

It isn't necessarily better to have music or story time in the morning rather than in the afternoon. Teachers in each class choose what seems best for their group, and sometimes things are switched around. However, there are certain principles you should look for in any posted schedule, which demonstrate that teachers are planning thoughtfully.

ALTERNATING DIFFERENT TYPES OF ACTIVITIES

Throughout each day, from the toddler class on up to pre-k, there are several types of activities that should be scheduled to alternate with each other:

Large and Small Muscle Activities

Gross motor and fine motor activities should alternate. If older preschoolers were scheduled to move from an extended outdoor playtime directly to a half-hour exercise or dance class, you can see that they could become too physically tired for an optimal experience with each. In the same way, if they work at the art table for fifteen or twenty minutes, followed immediately by time at the manipulative materials table, and then went right to computer class, this could cause a different kind of fatigue.

Louder and Quieter Activities

By the same token, louder activities need to alternate with quieter ones. Too much time spent in either type of activity is not best. Longer outdoor playtimes or inside gym periods, times when children engage in vigorous play and use louder voices, can cause physical fatigue, which can lead to emotional fatigue. And expecting young children to remain engaged in quiet activities that last too long is not appropriate, either. They need freedom to get up and move around, to talk freely with their friends, and to laugh and sing spontaneously.

Child-Directed and Teacher-Directed Activities

Periods when children are free to choose and direct their own activity should alternate with times when teachers are leading these choices. If teachers failed to exercise appropriate leadership, most children would feel some distress and tension by midmorning, and returning to a more relaxed atmosphere could be challenging. Children must be free to make meaningful choices for themselves. But if left on their own to choose how to spend their time all day long, without guidance from adults, the quality of most children's day would quickly deteriorate. Meaningful choice includes decisions children are sufficiently mature to handle. The nature of the group dynamic of a preschool class requires that extended periods of free choice be limited by alternating with other activities, where the responsibility for choosing what to do next is removed from the child for a time.

> MEANINGFUL CHOICE INCLUDES DECISIONS CHILDREN ARE SUFFICIENTLY MATURE TO HANDLE.

12

FIELD TRIPS AND EXTRACURRICULAR ACTIVITIES

On a beautiful spring day early in my tenure as a child care provider, a group of our older four-year-olds went on a field trip to a local strawberry patch. The trip was a natural extension of their topic of discussion for several weeks—"Life on a Farm." Everybody was very excited, and we had plenty of adults to supervise the group, including several parents who were helping us transport the children to a suburb south of Nashville. The children had all brought sack lunches and were looking forward to a picnic at the farm, after first picking strawberries to take home.

The trip down was uneventful, and the picking began in earnest as soon as we arrived. The children, teachers, and parents were all very enthusiastic about this experience. The temperature was moderate and the skies partly cloudy. Perfect weather for picking strawberries. Little did we know that several miles north, a thunderstorm had popped up, and our center was in its path.

The storm knocked out the center's electricity, and while it was out for only a little while, our phone system was dependent on power to work. (This was before cell phones.)

We discovered the problem with the phones when one of our children was stung by a bee. Unfortunately, his parents were not among the group accompanying us that day. Using the farm's telephone, we were unable to reach the center to get his parents' work numbers.

The good news was that the farmer had tobacco, which we mixed with water to make a paste to relieve the pain of the sting. The even better news was that this child was not allergic to bee stings.

I learned an important lesson that day. From then on, whenever we took our children beyond the bounds of our little campus, we always brought along copies of important information from the file of each child, including medical treatment authorizations and parent contact numbers.

PERIODICALLY, CAREGIVERS WILL TAKE THEIR PREschoolers on fields trips. When children are informed of these plans, they're always enthusiastic and excited. Field trips afford some delightful opportunities and experiences for children, but it is very important that they are properly planned and executed. Failure to do so could place children at risk.

FIELD TRIPS

Logistical planning

It would be very difficult for a center's staff members to pull off an effective field trip with preschoolers on their own. We always asked for, and were fortunate to receive, the help of parents.

Any time preschool children are taken out of the controlled environment of center facilities, there are some obvious areas of vulnerability. Others are not so obvious. Some member(s) of the center staff need to go ahead of the group prior to field trip day to determine potential risks for young children. Even when a particular venue has been

Field Trips and Extracurricular Activities

visited before, sometimes entrances and parking area configurations change. It's important to recognize that what worked well last year may not be the same this year. For the protection of children, someone must think all these issues through for each field trip experience.

How far will children have to walk to enter the venue? Is there an area where vehicles can pull up to the curb adjacent to the entrance? Where is the safest point of crossing? If a van is being used, who will help children out of their car seats and off the van, while others wait to hold hands and someone else opens entrance doors? Where are the restrooms, and who will supervise the child who needs to use the restroom while others are enjoying the event? Children cannot be left alone for even a moment at school, and certainly not in a public place.

Transportation methods

Sometimes centers have a bus or van used for transporting school-age children to and from grade school. When such vans are outfitted with appropriate child safety seats, they can work for preschoolers. However, it is important that there are extra adults present because of the behavioral limitations of preschool children. State laws may require that an adult other than the driver be present when a certain number of preschoolers are transported. However, merely abiding by the regulations may not provide adequate protection. Additional adults may be necessary, depending on the circumstance.

> FOR THE PROTECTION OF CHILDREN, SOMEONE MUST THINK ALL THESE ISSUES THROUGH FOR EACH FIELD TRIP EXPERIENCE.

Often we used parents' and staff members' personal vehicles. Our state requires that centers keep a copy of the driver's license and proof of automobile insurance on file for any person who transports enrolled children. Parents and staff were always glad to provide these.

On the morning of field trip day, parents who were not going on the trip left their child's safety seat at the center so these could be used in the cars of those who would be driving. It's important that each driver recognizes there will be safety seats of every brand and type imaginable. Each car seat must be properly installed. At times a call to Mom or Dad at work may be necessary to ensure this is correctly done. Extra time must be figured into the plan to allow for this possibility.

Safety first

We ultimately decided to take a field trip only if each adult, whether a caregiver or a parent, had only two specific children to supervise. This allowed the adults to hold the hand of each child they were responsible for whenever necessary. We didn't consider this to be "overkill" because it made us all feel better. The adults had much more fun on the trips than we would have if we each had four children to watch.

Preschoolers cannot be relied on to recognize potential dangers. And since their attention spans are brief, they are easily distracted. A preschool child might wander off if the supervising adult glances away for a moment. Often the venues we visited were also being visited by other preschools. At times there were many children present. Whether we were visiting the children's museum or a pumpkin farm, with two children per adult, we were assured of appropriate monitoring and supervision.

An additional safety device we often used on field trips was that all the children wore a brightly colored T-shirt, all of the same color, with our center's name printed on it. Also, we were careful about how we scheduled our time on field trips so children didn't become overstimulated or tired.

EXTRACURRICULAR ACTIVITIES

Centers often offer additional enrichment programs for children beyond what the basic curriculum provides. Parents may choose whether or not their child will participate in these. These programs typically involve an additional fee, paid to an outside service provider. Sometimes extracurricular programs are provided on-site. Others require transporting children to an off-site location, which may necessitate a transportation fee to cover additional costs incurred by the center, such as vehicle insurance, fuel, and extra staffing costs.

What kinds of classes are offered?

Our program offered several extracurricular opportunities. Among these were ballet and swimming classes, which were offered off-site. At various times, some of our on-site classes also included French; Spanish; basic signing for the hearing impaired; and computer, gymnastics, and performing arts classes.

Children who don't participate

There were always some children from each preschool class who participated in one or several of our extracurricular activities while others did not. Sometimes a child couldn't participate due to a disability. Sometimes parents chose not to incur this additional expense. Thoughtful teachers guard against anyone feeling "left out" by providing special in-class activities during these periods.

13

FOOD SERVICE

avannah Kingsley's mouth dropped open when I said that her three-year-old had eaten broccoli for lunch that day. Parker was a very picky eater, as preschoolers often are, but she had eaten all of the lunch Ms. Annabelle had served. As she was bringing lunch in, Ms. Annabelle explained to the children that she knew they had been talking a lot about the color green, since spring had come. She told them she had added green dots of broccoli to their macaroni and cheese—"for pretty." Our cook was always finding creative ways of introducing new foods. We all loved Ms. Annabelle.

MEALS PROVIDED, INCLUDED IN TUITION

All full-day child care centers and family day homes are responsible for feeding the children at appropriate intervals throughout the day. Some provide hot lunch service in addition to midmorning and midafternoon snacks. Certain centers also provide breakfast. A late-afternoon snack may be provided for those children whose parents arrive near closing time and whose dinner will be served later than most. The cost of most meals is usually included in your tuition. The exception might be the cost of breakfast, which may require an additional fee.

WHO PREPARES THE FOOD?

Many centers that provide hot meals prepare them on-site in their own kitchens. In a large center, a cook is designated to plan for and prepare these meals, with the director's oversight. Other centers have meals prepared off-site, with food delivered by a caterer. Simple midmorning and midafternoon snacks are usually prepared on-site.

WHO PLANS THE MENUS?

Our program had a nutritionist work with our cook to develop and periodically revise our menus. This ensured that children were offered a balanced, nutritious diet at school. Menus were rotated so that no particular menu was repeated more often than every four or five weeks. Some of our creative cooks liked to schedule menu changes to provide even greater variety.

We provided sufficient food and milk to be certain that each child could have extra servings until satisfied. Food service planning should always consider this need of growing children.

LUNCH BOXES FROM HOME

Many programs require parents to bring lunch from home. Certain states require directors to provide parents with nutritional guidelines for acceptable lunch box menus for children enrolled in a state-licensed facility. A representative of the state agency that regulates the program periodically stops in for unannounced visits at lunchtime to ensure that foods children bring from home meet the requirements of the state's nutritional guidelines.

BRINGING IN BREAKFAST

Because our program did not provide breakfast, we made sure that the midmorning snack was ample for children who may have rushed through their breakfast at home. We requested that parents serve breakfast before coming to school rather than sending breakfast into the classrooms with their children in the mornings. If this were to happen, it could present a hardship for the child who doesn't get to have jelly donuts.

SPECIAL DIETS: ALLERGIES & RELIGIOUS REQUIREMENTS

Sometimes children had special dietary requirements due to allergies or religious customs, which we followed carefully. We worked with parents who kept special watch over the center's menus, along with our center's staff. We wanted to be sure that either we or they provided extra food on a day when the menu offered a dish that was banned for that child.

LUNCHTIME IN THE CLASSROOM

Some programs offer a separate lunchroom for meal service, but often children dine at tables in their own classroom. Teachers in toddler and preschool classes are careful to sanitize table surfaces before and after each meal, just as infant caregivers do with high chairs in the nursery. Children are taught and helped with adequate hand-washing techniques, as needed. They learn to rub in the soap until it makes bubbles, taking time to ensure effective cleansing.

Teachers often designate a mealtime helper each week, rotating through all the children over time. After washing their hands, these children help to set the table for lunch. When the meal is over, each preschooler learns to help with cleanup by throwing away his own paper plate and cup.

GIVING THANKS

At our center, we had a simple prayer before each meal, to thank the Giver of the food. We learned through parents that many children who enjoyed having prayer before meals at school began to lead their families to give thanks before meals at home. Everyone in our parent group knew that this was our practice before they enrolled. They all seemed to appreciate the value of their child learning to be thankful for blessings.

ARE PARENTS WELCOME FOR LUNCH?

Our parents had a standing invitation to join their child's class for lunch. All we asked was that they inform us ahead of time so we could prepare extra food in case several parents came on the same day.

14

EMERGENCY PREPAREDNESS

ne of our large classrooms had floor-to-ceiling windows with views onto the front lawn and driveway. All three of our preschool classes had been invited to come into the room to stand in front of the window wall for just a few minutes. No one wanted to miss what was about to happen. As they had graciously done before, the staff of a nearby fire station had agreed to come over to talk with the children about fire safety. They were bringing the big red truck and several firemen dressed in their firefighting gear. Here in front of the windows, everyone could watch the fire truck's arrival.

When we told the children the firemen had called to say they were on their way, the excitement in the room intensified. And when they heard the sound of the big engine approaching, all of the children took a little gasping breath. They were all, in a word, awestruck. As the vehicle pulled into view and approached the driveway, the driver sounded the siren briefly. Everybody squealed and shouted at once. The energy coming from that group of little people was a sight to behold.

Once the truck was safely stopped and parked, the children, their caregivers, and a few parents walked outside for a closer look. The children listened intently as the men told them about the various features of the vehicle and of their uniforms, and why these were important in helping to put out a fire. Afterward, each child was given a red fire hat of their very own to take home. They all gained new respect for these emergency workers that day, as did all of their grown-up friends.

PART OF THE JOB OF CHILD CARE CENTER STAFF IS TO BE prepared in the event of an emergency. Everyone hopes and prays that they will never be faced with such an incident; however, staff must plan ahead and be prepared.

PREPARING CHILDREN TO LISTEN

One of the most important ways that staff can prepare children for an emergency is through how they manage their class every day. Children who are accustomed to attentive caregivers listening to them also learn to listen to their caregivers. These children come to love their teacher and respect her leadership. When the teacher speaks to them in a certain tone, saying, "We need to all walk outside right now," they are much more likely to understand something important is happening and to obey this directive. Teachers who take this approach are actually preparing their children for an emergency every day, including each time they walk out onto their playground in an orderly way.

Children whose caregivers are not very responsive to them as individuals probably won't respond to their teacher in the same way. Unfortunately, when their needs for individual attention are not being met by the person they are depending on for such attention, little resentments and rebellions can develop. These attitudes could be an obstacle in an emergency, when children need to follow clear directions for the safety of all.

MEETING FIREMEN AND POLICE OFFICERS

Periodically, our staff would have Community Helpers Week. Among the helpers who would visit were certain emergency workers. In addition to seeing fire engines and firemen, children met police officers, too. They briefly sounded their sirens for children to hear. These events were exciting for our preschoolers, who had all kinds of questions for these folks.

EMERGENCY DRILLS

Children can understand that we have fire drills to keep us safe. Our classrooms had direct access to the outdoors, so it was possible to evacuate one hundred thirty children from our large, multibuilding facility in forty-five seconds. This included the time it took to evacuate all infants and toddlers. We sounded our fire alarm system when we had fire drills so children would learn that the alarm meant we were all going outside. Our system was connected to the fire station, so we always called to let them know we were about to have a drill. In a real emergency, they would know immediately if we were in distress.

> STAFF PREPARE CHILDREN FOR AN EMERGENCY THROUGH THE WAY THEY MANAGE THEIR CLASS EVERY DAY.

MEETING DOCTORS AND NURSES

Children who meet doctors and nurses at preschool while in a group of other young children are much less likely to be fearful when they visit the doctor or dentist. This is especially true when these health care workers are the parents of their classmates. Having experienced a brief visit from a health care worker during "Healthy Living" week could mean a lot to the child who was required to meet his parents at the hospital emergency room, surrounded by people in white coats.

Our emergency plan/procedure for a child's serious illness or injury that required emergency room care included phone calls, in the following order: First, call 911 to request an ambulance. Second, call the hospital emergency room. We wanted to make ourselves available to ER staff to answer any question they might have that EMS could not answer. Third, call the parents to let them know what was happening and where to meet us, making every effort to avoid alarming them. The parent would probably be driving themselves to the hospital.

Our plan provided for the child's primary caregiver to go with the child on the ambulance to reassure and calm the child. An administrative staff member or other substitute would take that caregiver's place in the classroom, reassuring and calming any children who might have become aware of a situation that could cause concern or fear.

MEDICAL RECORDS AND TREATMENT AUTHORIZATION

As mentioned in the chapter on field trips, after the strawberry picking/bee sting incident, any time we removed a child from center property, whether for a field trip, a swim or ballet class, or any other reason, caregivers carried a copy of the child's latest health record. This record included contact information for his pediatrician. We also took the document by which parents had authorized us to procure any needed emergency care as well as all contact information for parents and their emergency contact designees.

NATURAL DISASTER

In 1998 a series of tornadoes hit Nashville, Tennessee. One of them was a Category F5. When the weather service placed our city under a tornado warning, our staff moved all the children, including the babies, to our basement. While the storm raged close by, over one hundred small children sat quietly with their teachers in the basement of our preschool, waiting out the storm. The remarkable thing about this was the amazing degree of calm that pervaded that space. It testified to the caliber of women who were working in our center. There was a lot of damage to large downtown buildings and neighborhoods near our location, but we were spared physical harm to persons or damage to our facility. And children were spared the psychological trauma that could have resulted if teachers had succumbed to their personal fears, failing to put children and their needs for reassurance first.

> THE CALM THAT PERVADED THAT SPACE TESTIFIED TO THE CALIBER OF WOMEN WORKING IN OUR CENTER.

Tennessee requires child care centers to prepare to house and feed children overnight in the event of a natural disaster. If a bad ice storm were to hit our city, parents might be unable to reach their children. We were prepared with extra blankets and food for such a possibility. Additionally, we had a "sister" center within walking distance, with which we had arranged reciprocal support if any emergency ever rendered one or the other of our buildings uninhabitable. We would also rely on the police department to help escort our group if we were ever forced to move all of our children.

PART FIVE

Community–A Pathway to Peace

15

YOUR NEW WAY OF LIFE

Over the first several weeks that Jennifer Hawthorne's infant was enrolled in our program, Jennifer's every movement, facial expression, and word betrayed her response to all of us that she was "fine." She looked as though a strong gust of wind could have broken her. I knew that she likely cried all the way to work, and again through the traffic, all the way back to the center each afternoon. And at each end of her commute to and from work, she told me later, she "got herself together" so she could appear to coworkers and center staff to be "fine." She exhibited all the signs of the profound grief of this loss that I myself had known.

I regretted that Jennifer had not taken full advantage of our invitation to schedule several visits in the nursery before her child's first day. She did come in on two occasions but left almost immediately each time. It was as if just being present there was forcing this mom to live through the painful coming separation from her baby before it actually occurred. In her desire to put off this difficulty as long as possible, she missed some experiences that could have been quite helpful to her.

Finally, however, as the weeks rolled on, she began to relax somewhat. Little Anna was doing well. The baby was calm and content throughout the day, including when her mom arrived each afternoon, and she was sleeping and eating well at home.

The contentedness of the other babies in the nursery also began to sink in for Jennifer. More and more as she came and went each day, she saw that other infants in the room were comfortable with their caregivers, enjoying the women's company and attention. They seemed happy and at ease in the setting. She began watching, in those children's behaviors, some of the things Anna would be able to do in only a few more months, observing those who had begun to crawl, pull up, or speak in "baby talk."

WHEN YOUR CHILD IS ENROLLED IN A CHILD DEVELOPMENT program, your family is embarking on a new way of life. There are many exciting possibilities, as well as some vulnerabilities, inherent in this. You want to make the transition for your child and yourself as smooth as possible. In a quality program, there will be a group of people who stand ready to do everything they can to help.

Ideally, your child will have several visits to his or her new center before the first full day of care. It is well worth your effort to make this happen, since the investment of time this takes will prove very beneficial to your child and so to you. When parents decided to enroll their child in our program, we recommended a visit schedule and expected visits from them.

YOUR BABY'S ADJUSTMENT TO DAY CARE

For parents of infants, the time of day for these visits did not have much significance. The purpose of visiting with babies was more for the adults than for the babies, especially the younger ones. Caregivers needed the opportunity to be with the baby a little before the first day.

During these visits, parents and staff had opportunities to begin getting to know one another. They could talk about what the infant's day was like at home. Mothers were asked to write down as much information as they felt important to give to nursery staff. This firsthand information helped staff members as they got to better know this baby. Upon enrollment in the center, the staff would always endeavor to maintain the same schedule and experiences the baby was used to at home.

> IN A QUALITY PROGRAM, THERE WILL BE A GROUP OF PEOPLE WHO STAND READY TO DO EVERYTHING THEY CAN TO HELP.

Caregivers also got to observe mother and child together, learning about the baby's preferences in simple things such as preparation for sleep routines or ways she prefers being held. Mothers got to see our caregivers hold, feed, and talk to their baby. They also had the benefit of closely observing caregivers' interactive care of the other infants in the nursery. Watching the other babies' needs being met lovingly, calmly, and effectively was reassuring for these new moms. They realized that this was a good place for their baby to be, which naturally relieved a lot of their anxiety about the coming separation.

Finally, on their second or third pre-enrollment visit, we invited new mothers to leave the baby with us for an hour or so. Running an errand or visiting the hair salon, then returning to discover that her child was fine made the first full day's good-bye much easier than it was for mothers who never took advantage of this more gradual approach.

YOUR TODDLER'S OR PRESCHOOLER'S ADJUSTMENT

Visit schedules for toddlers and preschoolers seemed to work best in our center when the first visit took place midafternoon. When the newly enrolling child comes in with Mom or Dad at this time, he enters into one of the least structured times of the children's day. The new classmates will have had a nap and most will have finished toileting routines. The class will have the feel of a family home, just with lots more children. People will be looking forward to snack time and, on nice days, to some outdoor play.

Typically the "new" child walks out to the playground, holding Mom or Dad's hand. He hovers around Mom or Dad for a while, feeling a little uncertain of all this newness. As his parent(s) enjoy a casual visit with caregivers, he watches the other children play. He may or may not participate on this day. Different children need different amounts of observation time, and it's best not to push them to participate.

> SEVERAL PRE-ENROLLMENT VISITS MAKE ENROLLING MUCH EASIER FOR YOU AND YOUR CHILD.

If the parent walks over to look at a particular piece of play equipment, he'll likely follow along. The child responds to his parent's signal that these are nice people and this is a fun place to be. But don't be surprised if he's a little shy or "clingy" on the first visit or so.

As parents become more relaxed in the environment, so does the new child. He begins to feel free to explore a little, and as he does this discovers a lot of interesting play opportunities. These motivate him to try more new things. Soon he finds himself playing alongside one of his new classmates. The new classmates are interested in the new child, too, gradually giving him more and more signals that he is welcome.

On the next pre-enrollment visit, we encouraged parents to again come with their child for an hour or so, this time at midmorning. On this occasion, children are in their classroom, working in activity centers. Beginning the second visit at a period when children were indoors rather than out on the playground but still free to choose their own activities served important purposes: The new child was able to experience another nonthreatening in-class period. Although he was inside his new classroom and in the presence of new classmates, he did not feel pressure to participate in a more structured whole-group activity the moment he walked in the door. That could be threatening to a child who hadn't experienced this before.

Rather than immediately facing a teacher-directed group activity, he got to have a good look at the toys and equipment available in his new class. At the same time he could freely observe how the other children were enjoying themselves here. Then, when the teacher called the group over for music, he might go sit with the others or stay close to Mom and Dad, observing this from a distance.

Ideally this period would be followed by another outdoor play period. By this time, the child usually would be ready to go farther out into the playground, becoming more involved with the others than he was on the previous visit. And we always encouraged parents to end their visit before outdoor time ended, taking their child by the hand and saying good-bye to new teachers and classmates. Always leave them wanting more!

On the next visit, the child would usually stay at the center on his own, without Mom and Dad. The time frame here would again be at least an hour or so, scheduled at mid to late morning. We always tried to arrange for the new child to enjoy whatever classroom and/or playground activities were taking place, and then stay for lunch. Mom or Dad would pick him up after lunch and before nap. Preferably, he would be able to observe children comfortably preparing for nap before leaving with his parents.

> AS YOU BECOME MORE RELAXED IN THIS ENVIRONMENT, SO DOES YOUR CHILD.

The child who was allowed this gradual entrance into center life usually was much better prepared for the first full day away from Mom and Dad than the child who had never had these preliminary experiences. You can see how a series of visits like this would be of significant benefit to your child.

YOUR OWN ADJUSTMENT TO DAY CARE

This is a very personal thing. We talked before about some of the inevitable, difficult emotions that accompany this new experience. Each parent comes to terms with these in the solitude of her own heart.

There will also be some positive emotions for you. Over time as you see your child adjusting well to school, you will experience a great sense of relief, realizing that you have found a good, healthy situation for him or her.

Your child's tears are different from your own

> THIS IS A VERY PERSONAL THING.

It helps to know that while your child will miss you, he will not be experiencing the same grief that is typical for mothers who are adjusting to this separation. That is because he is not capable of the bigger-picture perspective that forms the foundation of this challenge for you.

Typically, a new child will have periods throughout the early days, usually brief in actual measured time, when he will miss his parent(s) and the way things were before. He may cry. There may be some sadness and possibly even anger about this. After all, the child didn't make this decision and wasn't really even consulted.

Staff members are sensitive to this period of adjustment in children. They are there to give encouragement and a hug when needed. A caregiver could never take a mother or father's place, but your child gains a new friend in his teacher. Caregivers will engage him in play, both with themselves and with other children. Soon all the fun, interesting activities going on take over his interest.

The child's orientation to time

The number of hours you will spend away from your child in day care are significant. You'll probably find yourself thinking about how she is doing and missing her throughout your workday for some time to come. It helps to realize that the young child's orientation to time is different from your own.

Children live very much in the present. When focused on a particular toy or new friend or activity, they give this their entire attention. The capacity to do this is part of why they're able to learn so much so fast in their early years. Once again, the brief attention spans of young children are working in your favor.

It is a rare preschooler who cannot be distracted from missing Mommy through the attraction of so many interesting things to do at school. While most children experience some rough patches for the first few days or even week or so, their natural curiosity will win the day. Soon you'll recognize that he is spending productive time while away from you. He'll be making new friends, learning new things, growing in social and emotional maturity and enjoying his new way of life. When this happens, the burden you have been carrying for your little person's transition into this new life will be lifted from your heart. You'll then be free to accept it for yourself.

SEPARATION ANXIETY

Every child in day care will have a hard time saying good-bye at times. This is true even for children who have spent several years in a preschool they love and in which they feel completely at home. Just as you wish some mornings that you could sleep in for a few more minutes and spend a relaxed morning in the peace and quiet of home, the child who is fully integrated into a program may feel this way sometimes, too.

Separation anxiety in the child's adjustment period to a new center is a little different. Here the child is aware of all the newness of this experience and may feel overwhelmed by it all. Tears can be the natural result. Sometimes it helps for parents to spend a little extra time in the morning in the classroom or nursery. Some children enter into play more readily while parents are present. Once they become engaged in play, on their own or with other children, they're ready for you to leave. All that's needed is a good-bye hug.

Other children may do better when parents stay only a few moments, assuring them that they're going to have a great day and that they'll see them this afternoon after work. Then they say good-bye and leave. This may result in loud cries of protest. For some, it's best to just say your confident good-bye, then walk out the door, trusting that caregivers will intervene to distract and lead your child into play.

Often when a parent makes efforts to reason with the child that he really doesn't need to cry, this only causes the child to become more entrenched in the tears. You get the sense, in some cases, that there's less sorrow and more battle of the wills going on. If that has become the case, it really is better for the parent to just leave. Anything else merely prolongs the agony. A child who is trying to control things for Mom or Dad is smart enough to realize that once his parent has left the building, he's wasting his time. And there's so much interesting stuff to do.

> STAFF MEMBERS MAKE SURE YOU KNOW ABOUT ACTIVITIES PLANNED FOR EACH DAY.

If your child continues having trouble separating from you in the mornings, this naturally causes more separation anxiety for you. Be assured that it is important to staff members to help out with this problem. If the child's adjustment to school is good throughout the day, excepting the morning good-bye, there will probably be a relatively quick fix for this problem.

If separation problems are more intense or prolonged than you would expect, set aside time to talk with your primary caregiver or the program's director. The director may suggest that you linger a while in the classroom at afternoon pick-up time for several days so your child can see you there, relaxed and talking with his teachers and classmates, just enjoying being with them. (Some parents continue this practice throughout the day care years, not because the child is having difficulty separating, but simply to be more a part of their child's life at school.) Together, the adults in this child's world can formulate the best approach to help him work through this period.

"WHAT DID YOU DO AT SCHOOL TODAY?"

It is important to talk with your preschooler about his or her day at school. But many parents have told me that when they ask the question above, the answer they get is, "Nothing." There could be several reasons why the child might respond this way.

So much goes on at school each day that children are drained. They've been interacting with others all day long and may be tired of talking. Or they may have had such a variety of experiences that they don't know where to begin.

> THERE ARE MANY WAYS FOR PARENTS TO BE A PART OF THEIR CHILD'S LIFE AT SCHOOL.

In a good child development program, staff members will make sure you are kept informed of what is going on each day. This will include what topic your preschooler's or toddler's class is focusing on this week and many of the planned activities related to that. You will be informed where the schedule and activities for each day of the week are posted. You may be given a copy to take home with you.

If your child is studying dinosaurs this week, one activity may be "an archaeological dig" in which children take turns searching for dinosaur bones in a sandbox, using little shovels. Teachers paint small twigs or bone-shaped doggy treats with white paint and bury them in dirt or sand. Children have the fun of discovering bones of extinct creatures.

When you know that this activity took place on a particular day, you might ask, "Did anybody find a dinosaur bone today?" This kind of question will probably elicit an enthusiastic response, with many details of your child's experience. You'll get your child's sense of the fun and excitement of this event.

If there was a problem with another child who wanted to claim the bones your child found, you'll probably hear about that, too. You'll be able to offer guidance about how he can work this out with his friend or their teacher.

Over time as your child talks about school, you will learn the names of his new friends and some things about them. You'll begin to put names and faces together as you come and go each morning and afternoon. This allows you to become more a part of your child's day at school. Children of parents who take time for this kind of involvement gain increased confidence and security in their preschool environment and in themselves.

16

A COMMUNITY OF FRIENDS

ne morning when Anna was about six months old, Jennifer Hawthorne walked into the nursery with a big smile on her face. She handed Ms. Betty a shiny red apple. At home that morning, Jennifer told us she realized that Anna might like to bring an apple for her teacher.

On this day, it was evident that Jennifer had turned an important corner. We knew she still wished, like most mothers do, that she could be home with her child during this early period of Anna's life. But Jennifer was assured that if that wasn't possible (and for Jennifer, it was not possible), she could be secure in knowing that she had found a good place for her baby. She was confident the people in our center cared deeply about Anna and could be trusted to protect her best interests every day.

IT IS PERFECTLY NATURAL FOR A PARENT WHO MUST choose child day care services to feel all kinds of difficult emotions. If you are facing some of these right now, you're not alone. Whether you have never used day care before and are just beginning to search for a center, or you have already found your center and continue to feel uncertain about your decision, there are some factors that can enable you to resolve this emotional distress.

PROTECTING TREASURE

Imagine for a moment that you are a member of a family that possesses a treasured heirloom, an irreplaceable diamond ring passed down for several generations. This ring has been worn by women in your family, including your beloved grandmother. You have just learned that the family has chosen you to be the keeper of this treasure during your lifetime. When you grow old, the ring will be passed on to some member of the next generation. With joy and pride, this gift is presented to you by the people you love most.

Now suppose that you are unable to wear the ring. You make your living working with your hands, creating delicate embroidery. As hard as you try, you just can't get accustomed to it. And you cannot give it back. You are the appropriate female family member. Guarding this ring is your responsibility.

Maybe you could put it in a safe somewhere in your house. But what if a thief broke in and stole it? Or you might take it to a local art gallery to be kept in a case for people to look at and enjoy. But while the gallery has a good reputation, you feel unsure. If the ring was kept in a locked box at the bank, it would probably be safe there, but then who would be able to enjoy it?

The answer to this challenge is similar to the answer you need in order to find peace with child care. You need someone you can count on—someone who cares enough to view your interests as her own. What you really need to help you protect a treasure, is a friend.

FEAR VERSUS REASON

When you first enroll your child into a child development program, you probably don't know anyone very well. The people who will be caring for your child really are strangers to you. You probably have a feeling that these are nice people, or you wouldn't have chosen this center, but you don't know for sure. You may wonder what they're like when you leave. When you toured the program, was their kindness and concern all just a show, or was it real?

If you are really anxious and uncomfortable about leaving your child with these people every morning, you might avoid getting to know them better. If you are apprehensive about these persons in your heart, you will not want to know them, for fear you might be proven right. If you are right and they are not worthy of your trust, what will you do then? You have to work and this was the very best choice you could have made.

> EVERY FRIEND YOU'VE EVER KNOWN WAS FIRST A STRANGER.

Without thinking this through, you, like Jennifer Hawthorne, may think that avoidance is your best defense. Maybe it's best not to know the truth. If these people are untrustworthy, maybe it's best for you to just continue on hoping that nothing bad happens. Otherwise, if you find out that they are not good people, you will have to take some action and you don't know what that would be. It's probably best not to get too close to them.

Allowing fear to govern our emotions diminishes our ability to reason. The mother who is in this position can miss the very thing that would be her salvation. Her child's teachers may be reaching out to her in little ways every day, but she doesn't notice. She can't see their efforts of kindness because, tragically, fear has built a wall between her and her child's caregivers. And she may be looking for anything that could be wrong with her child, missing everything that's right.

CULTIVATING FRIENDSHIPS

Every friend you've ever had was first a stranger. Whether it's someone you know socially or a neighbor or coworker, you had to move forward in a relationship with someone new with some measure of faith. At first you had to give that person the benefit of the doubt. As time went on, she proved herself trustworthy.

So it is now. You have made the difficult analysis of your family's true need and decided that you must have child care services. You have toured programs and made the best choice available to you, within your personal resources. Now you are entering this new way of life and must do another thing that may not be natural for you: give your child's caregivers the benefit of the doubt.

Doing this is harder for some people than for others. This is especially difficult for people who have experienced much disappointment or even betrayal in previous relationships with family and friends. Even so, for your child's sake, you must gather your courage for this worthy effort. You must make the decision to commit yourself to getting to know your child's caregivers.

Cultivating friendships with the caregivers is not like cultivating a social friendship. You probably won't be going out to dinner with these folks. Rather, it will be more like the friendship that develops with a trusted pediatrician or her nursing staff, who sees your child through a health crisis. Your friendship with caregivers will probably be within the scope of their professional service to your family. But that does not mean these individuals are not true friends to you.

Over time you will recognize their genuine, consistent concern for the well-being of children. And you will observe your child's natural response to this caring: a loving appreciation for his teacher.

In addition to the special kind of friendship you and your child enjoy together, he gains another adult friend and gains confidence in his world and in himself. Every time another adult in the center competently and lovingly engages in meeting your child's needs, he is strengthened more and more. He enters into a larger community of friends. Unless the program you have enrolled in is so structurally flawed that everyone on the staff is continually overloaded with more to do than is humanly possible, it is within your power to ensure that this happens for your child. This will be true in whatever center you have chosen. I am absolutely confident of this, because of my personal experience with caregivers over so many years.

YOUR OPPORTUNITY

The people who choose to do the difficult work of caring for young children and are able to sustain their efforts over time, have a special sensitivity and compassion for the very young. This capacity is a kind of spiritual giftedness in their lives—a gift not unlike that of an artist or of a counselor who works effectively with troubled teens. This heart orientation is present in them all the time, regardless of outward circumstances. It is this orientation of the heart that provides such wonderful potential for what your child can experience in their care.

This means that no matter what kind of center these caregivers work in, they have the ability to give of themselves to little children in ways that money cannot buy. It's just their natural way of being. So, when they work in a program that supports their efforts with generous provision of beautiful equipment and materials for children, they flourish. When they work in a program with financial constraints, requiring the constant use of ingenuity to provide rich experiences for their preschoolers, they flourish. This is what they do naturally because it brings them joy.

The truth is that there are programs in every community that don't yet provide the highest quality. They may not yet meet all the standards required for a high star rating or for accreditation. You may have had to choose one of these. Your center may not have all the latest toys and equipment and books. Your child's classroom may not have as much space as the center you wish you could have afforded. Its playground may not be as nice. Its curriculum may not seem to be as well thought through. But the director has shared some of their plans for increasing quality, and you see evidence of this in the pride and enthusiasm of staff members.

If you sense that the caregivers in this program seem to be enjoying their work and are comfortable in the company of children, take heart. You have found people who have within themselves the essence of what your child needs most in this experience. And within you lies the ability to encourage and strengthen them in this—to bring out their best for your child.

WHAT YOUR CHILD NEEDS MOST

Above all else in the time he spends away from you, your child needs a friend. He needs an adult companion on his journey through the preschool years, someone who will be focused on and interested in him every day. A friend who will provide interesting things to do and who will lead him to discover more and more about himself and the world around him. Someone who will be there for him, to guide and protect him. Someone who will be patient with him when he's having a hard day and testing her patience.

Your child needs an adult friend who will notice and give him a hug when he feels sad or afraid, and who will rejoice with him over his victories: when he is learning to stand alone, when he begins to exchange his bottle for a cup, when he begins to learn the joy of sharing. And later, when he fashions a building from modeling clay or tries and then conquers walking on the balance beam. Someone who will be proud of him on the day he recognizes a way to help someone else, reaching out in an effort to be a peacemaker between two of his classmates.

Just as there are programs of lesser technical quality, there are those recognized to have all the resources one could hope for in a child development program. All the bells and whistles. Just perfection. But if staff members are distracted, embroiled in gossip and strife, it isn't going to work the way it should. If the spirit of the staff is corrupted by jealousy or resentment, children will be diminished, because these attitudes among the caregivers will inevitably rain down upon them.

> EFFECTIVE CAREGIVERS HAVE SPECIAL COMPASSION FOR THE VERY YOUNG—A KIND OF SPIRITUAL GIFTEDNESS.

Despite having a beautiful, spacious building and your state's highest rating, if the individuals who work there are merely going through the motions of technically correct adult/child interaction, but their hearts are unengaged, they will fail your child. If the person or persons who interact one-on-one with your child every day seem distant and lack warmth toward him as an individual, all the rest of it won't make up for his loss.

What your child needs most in day care is free. It is a gift freely given from the heart of one who deeply cares for children. A good, truly loving relationship between your child and his caregiver(s) stands head and shoulders above every other aspect of your child's experience in day care.

BEFRIENDING YOUR CHILD'S FRIEND

One of my favorite scriptures provides an important key to successful relationships. It is found in the Bible, in the book of

Philippians, and says, "Whatever is true, whatever is honorable, whatever is right, whatever is pure, whatever is of good report, if there is any excellence, and if anything worthy of praise, let your mind dwell on these things."[1]

If you want to cultivate relationships that bring out the best in the persons who are going to have much influence on your child's early years, I invite you to reread the verse above. The principles contained there are worthy of serious consideration.

MISTAKES AS A CHALLENGE TO FRIENDSHIP

We've acknowledged that all persons are fallible. We all make mistakes at times. Sometimes we make a mistake due to circumstances that are quite beyond our control. For example: A mother has a note for her child's caregiver, instructing her to give her baby his afternoon juice bottle late today—a half hour later than regular juice time. Mom, who is new to life in the center, has forgotten that there is a "Special Instructions" sheet posted near the door, providing a secure place for such an instruction.

The caregiver is talking with another parent when the new mom comes in, and she doesn't want to interrupt. So she leaves the note on the countertop and goes on to work. As she exits the nursery, a little gust of wind blows the note off the counter into the trash can. The caregiver never sees the note, and the baby gets his juice at the usual time.

Later that afternoon, when Mom arrives, the afternoon staffer is talking with another parent. In her rush to keep up with this evening's schedule, Mom doesn't have time to wait for their conversation to end, so she hurriedly packs up her baby and leaves the nursery feeling frustrated. As she drives to her destination wondering whether the caregivers followed her instructions, her child starts to get fussy—letting her know that they did not give him his juice bottle when she asked, because he's already hungry now. Unfortunately, instead of going straight home, a ten-minute drive, tonight she will be meeting her husband at a restaurant, where they're having dinner with his parents. This requires a half hour of extra drive time. Although the baby's father will have stopped by the house to warm up a bottle, by the time she gets it from him, her hungry child will have moved beyond fussy—not a good start to this evening.

As she parks her car, the baby is now in full-blown disaster mode. Fussing has turned to loud cries of protest. Utter misery. Instead of impressing her in-laws with what a good mother she is, Mom feels like this situation proves the opposite. Now this new mom has to deal with the very thing she was trying to avoid. She is feeling ignored and disrespected by her child's caregivers, while at the same time feeling judged by her husband's parents.

If the caregiver had only followed her instructions, her baby would have been able to last that extra time until dinner. If these people don't have the flexibility to follow a simple instruction like waiting an extra half hour for juice time, how in the world can she trust them with her child? And since her primary caregiver had gone home by the time she picked up her baby, she couldn't even talk to her about this. The afternoon staffer obviously didn't notice that she needed to talk. What is wrong with these people?

Life has wrinkles

Neither the mother nor the caregiver is at fault here. This miscommunication occurred for two reasons: The mom, overwhelmed by her new way of life and unaccustomed to all its new systems, forgot about one of these systems. The caregiver was focused on another parent who was asking that staff be watchful for symptoms of illness, thinking her child might have been exposed through a neighbor. In her concern to fully understand one mother's instructions, the caregiver failed to properly greet the new mom.

Objective observation of this incident makes it clear that this is just one of life's wrinkles. No one is really at fault. The fact is this new mom is already in some degree of emotional distress. She's not fully healed from the sadness of having to be away from her baby all day. The emotions she's living with make her more vulnerable to what happened here than she would be if she had been enrolled in this program for a longer period of time.

The parents who have been in this program longer have developed trust in its staff. They've had time and experience that have allowed the caregivers to prove themselves trustworthy. This mom is still going on faith, hoping everything is going to work out but always looking for anything that might indicate otherwise.

If the same incident had occurred with a parent whose child had been enrolled longer, it would not have caused the same outcome: a potential crisis of relationship. But, unfortunately, it happened with a new mom.

The unfortunate, natural outcome

Everything this new mother did and everything she felt is perfectly natural. She was doing exactly what the staff told her they wanted her to do: communicate her needs to them. She was simply asking for a reasonable accommodation. Instead, she and her baby were seriously inconvenienced, and no one even apologized.

As people often do in similar circumstances, she may feel resentful and maybe even a little angry. And this new mom may not discuss this with the caregiver, waiting for her to make the first move, since, in her mind, she was the one at fault.

On the other hand, the caregiver has been sensing this new mother's continuing uncertainty toward her ever since she enrolled. This feels like a kind of judgment to this caregiver. While she has been holding, feeding, singing to, and generally "falling in love" with this new baby, just as she should, his mom seems to not even like her. She obviously doesn't even begin to notice, much less appreciate, all the caregiver does for her child.

The caregiver may be uncertain about what she should do. She feels the mother's judgment and doesn't know exactly how to resolve this problem. The afternoon staff member left the message that the new mom seemed upset yesterday, but she didn't know why. So the caregiver knows she needs to resolve a problem with this parent, but she doesn't really know what the problem is.

> SOMETHING ELSE NEEDS TO HAPPEN HERE SO THINGS CAN GET BACK ON TRACK.

If left up to the people involved, this miscommunication could naturally lead to ever increasing doubt, mistrust, and resentment on the part of everyone. If not dealt with directly, this mother may leave the program for another one, requiring yet another period of adjustment for her infant. Unfortunately, without a better understanding of how things really need to work in her relationship with staff members, she may have the same type of experience at the next center.

If the caregiver involved is relatively new to this work, she may feel as though she's done something really wrong. But she doesn't understand what. She may avoid talking with other long-term staff or with the director, fearing some reprisal or the loss of her job. While she may be very gifted for this work, she could easily become discouraged. As hard as she is trying to take good care of her four babies, one of their mothers clearly disapproves of her efforts. Maybe she's made a big mistake. Maybe the work she loves is not right for her after all.

Something else needs to happen here so things can get back on track. If everyone involved responds to this situation as they naturally feel inclined to do, it's easy to see the train wreck coming. To avoid this, someone must introduce an element of human behavior that doesn't come so naturally. Someone must choose to respond with mercy.

MERCY AND TODDLERS

Please allow me to refer back to something we discussed earlier: As a toddler enters that period when she starts becoming aware of her ability to exercise some degree of influence and control over her world, it is natural for her to feel good about this. She feels empowered as she has some success in this area. Then, when she bumps up against problems that constrain her ability to control things, it's just as natural for her to feel frustrated. Sometimes this frustration will result in a tantrum.

Any adult who lives or works with a two-year-old should expect that child to sometimes have tantrums. It's silly to expect otherwise. This is because of the developmental limits of the toddler's emotional capability. She can no more control her emotions at times than she could perform ballet in Swan Lake.

When we understand and expect a toddler to tantrum, it is far less threatening to us when it comes. It may be unpleasant, but we can respond to this behavior more appropriately because we know this is normal for a toddler. Understanding her behavioral limitations enables us to have compassion and kindness—mercy—toward the child. This truth gives us some freedom in this area.

MERCY AND ADULTS

When we try to cultivate a mutually respectful relationship with another person, we must be realistic. However intensely we want that person to always make right choices and do the right things, this is not a realistic expectation. Not even if she is our child's caregiver. Because this person is human. Just like we are.

We can know this about ourselves and others, but when reality collides with our expectations for a perfect morning, we tend to forget about this. It's natural for us, just like the toddler, to respond with frustration. And this is exactly where we all need to be careful.

Parents whose children are enrolled in day care and the center staff members who care for them need to understand a fundamental truth: The needs of the young child are more significant than their own personal needs for comfort and convenience. The adults in the child's world must behave responsibly. In the case of child care services, this means that more will be required of them in the area of interpersonal relationships than in many other areas of life.

> PARENTS AND CAREGIVERS NEED TO HOLD ONTO THE "BIG PICTURE" FOR EACH CHILD. WHAT IS BEST FOR HER?

In practice, this means that we don't have the freedom to react with our emotions. Rather, we need to respond to each other thoughtfully, with respect and kindness—quick to forgive when forgiveness is needed. This will not always be easy. It will be difficult, especially on days when our workload at the office is above and beyond us. It will be difficult when our caregiver makes a mistake, not out of a miscommunication, but due to a lapse in focus.

These are the times when caregivers and parents must give one another the benefit of the doubt. Judgments and blame, rather than understanding and forgiveness could result in the loss of what is really a valuable relationship for the child. Taking the natural course could result in the loss of a healthy friendship for him or her, coupled with the requirement of a brand-new transition into a new center, and all that entails.

Parents and staff members need to hold on to their vision of the "big picture" for each child. What is best for her? When we remove our focus from ourselves, our needs, and our rights, we're better able to see the child's needs. It's easier then to remember what, and who, this is all about. In that spirit, we're better able to weigh the value of our own personal sacrifice.

WHO IS THIS CAREGIVER, AND WHAT DOES SHE REALLY NEED?

The approach you take as you seek to cultivate a good relationship with your child's caregiver will make all the difference in its quality—whether it succeeds or fails. Just as it is important to understand some things about your child's developmental needs in order to make the right child care choice, understanding the caregiver's needs is important. Some insight into her perspective on her work will help you choose the right approach as you seek to know her better.

THE CAREGIVER'S ORIENTATION TO TIME

Just as your child's time orientation is different from your own, so, too, is the caregiver's. People who spend each workday in the company of young children and who are appropriately engaged with them have a unique perspective. In addition to their personal view of the world as a mature adult, they also view it through the eyes of the little children they are teaching and caring for. This is necessary if they are to effectively lead children into discovery. They must be sensitive to the child's perspective.

Preschool teachers develop understanding of each child's unique needs. They understand that one approach to helping a child develop socially works with one child but that another child may need something different. They learn children's likes and dislikes, their differing emotional limitations. Being this closely involved in each child's life brings about a unique and interesting point of view.

Little Things Mean a Lot: The Negative Effect

Good caregivers naturally want what is best for their children. Little things make a big difference. For example, the director schedules a visit by a ballerina. Out of the goodness of her heart, the dancer agrees to come on Friday to dance for the children, wearing a classic dance costume. The caregivers have prepared the children for this visit during their "Dancing and the Arts" week.

The children have looked at art books containing paintings of ballerinas, as well as contemporary photographs of the dancers. They have talked about how strong a ballerina must be to do her work. Some of the little girls are enthralled. Starry-eyed. Meeting a real ballerina is the only thing they talk about all week long. The boys are also interested in seeing what this lady can do.

On Thursday afternoon, the ballerina calls to say that she's made a mistake with her schedule. She meant to say she was available the following Friday.

In the course of ordinary life, this is really a fairly minor inconvenience. But in child care, it's huge. Children don't understand something like this very well. They're just hugely disappointed. And the caregiver, who is acutely aware of their loss, can offer no remedy. This kind of disappointment for children can become just about as significant for caregivers. This is one example of how a little disappointment, in the greater scheme of things, can be magnified in a child care center.

Little Things Mean a Lot: The Positive Effect

Happily, just as little things sometimes work in a negative way, they can also have a very positive effect. We were fortunate in our program. Most of our parent group recognized and really appreciated the work we were doing. From time to time, one of them would bring in a surprise for children. Sometimes they brought something just for staff members or just for their own child's caregiver(s).

The surprise for children might be leftover special colored card stock used in a print shop by a parent who worked there. This material would have been discarded, but the parent realized it could be put to good use in their child's art center.

Another surprise might come in the form of pretty scarves a mom had decided to give to a thrift shop. Instead she realized they would be put to good use in a home living activity center.

A dad might bring in fruit popsicles for a special afternoon snack for his child's class. A treat like this on a hot summer day was an unexpected piece of fun for everybody—children and caregivers alike. And sometimes a mom would bring her child's caregiver(s) a coffee from a specialty shop. Most preschool teachers can't afford such an extravagant treat.

KINDNESS BEGETS KINDNESS

When parents think of creative ways to express their respect and appreciation for the work of their child's caregivers, these simple acts of giving become huge blessings for the adults in the center. Whether it takes the form of little surprise gifts or is expressed through a word of genuine appreciation from time to time, this kind of thing is magnified in importance in the child care environment. And it tends to spread.

Kindness begets kindness. Soon more parents participate in acts of kindness toward the center staff and children. And from kindness comes joy. From joy comes an overflow of good things for your child. Community is forming.

All of us want our work to be appreciated. This is a normal, healthy desire. When a caregiver gives out of her heart to encourage a young child in her care, she has the reward of sensing the lasting value of what she has done. The preschool teacher who is mature and has strong integrity can go on doing this indefinitely, without any other reward. But how much better it is for her when the children's parents recognize what she's doing for their children and find ways to let her know they know!

Just as it is true for children, it is even more so for your child's teacher: this expression of gratitude cannot be faked. It must be genuine. But if you do see the value of what she brings to your child's life, tell her so from time to time. Her heart will be lifted up, and she will be refreshed. This will naturally result in even more good experiences for your child and her classmates.

> THE CAREGIVER HAS THE REWARD OF SENSING THE LASTING VALUE OF WHAT SHE HAS DONE.

THE POWER OF MERCY

In my personal life of faith in Christ, I have learned certain truths that have been liberating for me, one of them being that God loves me just the way I am, despite all the warts and wrinkles. He doesn't expect me to be perfect. He knows I'm not capable of that.

This means that when I fail at something, He still loves me. When my choices fly in the face of what I know He says is best and my actions bring dishonor, He still loves me. His love for me is not conditioned on what I do or don't do. God's love for me is unconditional, even at those times when I am angry at Him because things aren't working the way I want them to. When I screw up and break things, He takes the things I've broken and restores them. This has happened in my life many times. Each time I have experienced true mercy.

Earlier I said that the director of a strong child development program must be a person of mercy. Actually, this is needed in every person who has an impact on your child in day care. All the adults in the environment should be people who show mercy to others.

A good caregiver shows mercy to her children all day long. She has compassion toward them in their present state of development. She doesn't expect them to behave today the way she hopes they will as adults. She understands their interpersonal scrapes and spats and doesn't expect them to just stop being that way for her own convenience. She realizes they're going to spill things she will have to clean up. She knows why their emotions flare at times, when they don't yet have the words they need to express their feelings.

The good caregiver sets her heart upon each child in her class. She decides to do this for each child, because that is what they need.

> THIS IS HOW YOU WANT YOUR CHILD TO BE TREATED WHEN YOU CANNOT BE THERE YOURSELF.

This kind of thing has much deeper substance than mere affection. It has staying power, because it isn't dependent on how she feels at the moment. Lasting personal affection toward your child will come into her heart, but it will come after she makes this fundamental commitment to your child.

The effective caregiver always commits herself to doing what is best for each individual. This will include the times when the child is flying in the face of her rules, and times when children are angry at her. This is how you want your child to be treated by his caregiver(s) when you cannot be there yourself.

WHEN PEOPLE SHOW MERCY

Just as in all things human, we are imperfect in our ability to be compassionate and understanding—to offer mercy to others. This will be true for your child's caregivers as well. But when the adults in a center choose in their hearts to be merciful toward one another, they are deciding to allow one another to be human.

These adults move ahead in their relationships with one another, including staff-to-parent, parent-to-staff, staff-to-staff, and parent-to-parent relations, recognizing and accepting that everybody makes mistakes. Everybody has bad days. They decide to allow for this. While it will never work perfectly, the outcome will always be a far superior environment for children than what it would have been otherwise. Kindness begets kindness. Mercy begets mercy.

Encouraging your child's caregiver(s) in the day to day of child care center life has great potential for good. You can approach these individuals who perform countless acts of kindness toward your child with your own acts of kindness. When you show caring and consideration toward them as they do the difficult work of extending mercy to little children, it has a dynamic effect on their feelings about the work they do. Your involvement and support facilitates the true friendship you long for your child to have. Out of this friendship comes the peace you have been seeking: you now have confidence that your treasure is protected.

> THIS KIND OF THING HAS MUCH DEEPER SUBSTANCE THAN MERE AFFECTION. IT HAS STAYING POWER.

A Personal Note and a Prayer for Your Family

Dear Reader,

Over the course of twenty-seven years in my child development center, I had the opportunity to meet many new moms. Because we enrolled over two thousand families from all walks of life during that period, and because I personally spoke by phone with many more for whom we didn't have enrollment space, I am certain that the challenges addressed in *Peace with Child Care* are shared by most mothers looking for child care services. The commonality of the issues they were all facing was unmistakable.

I hope that reading *Peace with Child Care* has given you a deeper understanding of your child's needs in day care and has helped you discover your ability as a parent to significantly influence your program's environment. You may know someone who is struggling with these same difficulties, but who is reluctant to discuss her deepest concerns with anyone. If so, please consider lending her your book. Doing so may help her step out from the isolation she is feeling now into the awareness that many mothers before her have experienced the very same thing. Pointing her here could be very helpful, especially if she knows that it has helped you personally.

The positive influence of just one parent in a child care center adds joy to a caring environment. This inevitably affects not only that parent's child, but also every young child in that center in a very beneficial way. How much better it is, then, if even more parents in the center catch this vision.

If you believe in the message of *Peace with Child Care*, please help get the word out. We have included an information sheet near the end of the book for two other mothers, which includes our Web address. I believe the parents you tell will genuinely appreciate hearing about the book, so their child and their center can benefit from its information, too.

Finally, please allow me to share something very personal with you, as an older woman to a younger one. This is a statement of my personal faith and something I would say to you if I had the opportunity to meet you face-to-face.

As you contemplate the importance of extending the kindness of allowing the other adults in your child care center to "be human," always remember to let yourself be human, too. No one on this earth can be a perfect parent. The perfect life was lived by Someone else. He lived the perfect life and died the perfect death, so we no longer have to carry the weight of all that. Experiencing the pure, unconditional love and acceptance God offers changes how we look at ourselves and at others.

May the blessings of God be upon you and all those you love, and may you dwell in His perfect Peace.

> Truly yours,
>
> Jean

CHAPTER NOTES

Introduction

1. John 8:32 (English Standard Version of the Bible)

Chapter 2

1. Kathy Slobogin, "Day Care Dilemma: What's Best for Kids, Families?" May 2, 2001, http://edition.cnn.com/2001/fyi/teachers.ednews/05/01/day.care/index.html.

2. National Association of Child Care Resource and Referral Agencies, "Child Care in America." Accessed March 16, 2007, www.naccrra.org/policy/docs/childcareinamericafactsheet.doc.

3. N. Buckley, "AAMC Data Show Women Students Are the Majority Among Entrants to 40 Medical Schools," October 26, 1999. Press Release, American Association of Medical Colleges, www.aamc.org/newsroom/pressrel/1999/991026a.htm.

4. Dr. Ying Lowrey, "Women in Business: A Demographic Review of Women's Business Ownership." Research Summary, Office of Advocacy, U.S. Small Business Administration, p. 1, August 2006. For research summary, visit: www.sba.gov/advo/research/rs280.pdf; for the full report, visit: www.sba.gov/advo/research/rs280tot.pdf.

5. The Tax Foundation, "State and Local Tax Burdens by State, 1970-2006," April 12, 2006, www.taxfoundation.org/taxdata/show/335.html#burden_by_state-20060412.

6. Dubay, Curtis S., and Scott A. Hodge, "America Celebrates Tax Freedom Day," April 2006, www.taxfoundation.org/files/sr140.pdf.

7. TIME Magazine, "A Sub Prime Primer," March 15, 2007, www.time.com/time/magazine/article/0,9171,1599698,00.html.

8. Kathleen Kingsbury, "Pressure on Your Health Benefits," October 29, 2006, www.time.com/time/magazine/article/0,9171,1552040,00.html.

Chapter 3

1. Beth Talent (media contact), "'The Dave Ramsey Show' Adds 300th Station." Press Release, February 15, 2007, www.daveramsey.com/etc/cms/index.cfm?intContentID=6773.

CHAPTER 4

1. The Margaret S. Mahler Psychiatric Research Foundation, "Clinical Implications of Separation-Individuation Theory in Brief." Excerpted and adapted from M. Hossein Etezady, M.D., An Intergenerational Legacy: A Discussion of Anni Bergman's Paper, in S. Akhtar, ed. *Affect Development and Regulation During Separation-Individuation* (in press). Accessed March 17, 2007, www.margaretmahler.org/therapists/resources/papers/briefetazady.html.

2. Matthew Timm, "Behavioral Challenges with Preschoolers," *Special Education Leadership Magazine* (January–March 1993): 16–18.

3. Ibid.

4. Adaptation to foster emotional development of the children's song by Alfred B. Smith, "When You're Happy and You Know It," date unknown, http://en.wikipedia.org/wiki/If_You%27re_Happy_and_You_Know_It.

5. Matthew 7:12 (ESV)

CHAPTER 7

1. Sue Shellenbarger, "Finding Five-Star Child Care: States Rate Facilities in Effort to Boost Quality," *The Wall Street Journal* (March 23, 2006): D1.

2. For more on the FPG Child Development Institute, visit www.fpg.unc.edu/.
   For more about the Environment Rating Scales, visit www.fpg.unc.edu/~ecers/.

CHAPTER 9

1. Lynn Trimble, "Boosting Your Child's Brain Power," *Raising Arizona's Kids Magazine* (August 2002). Republished at http://mesaunitedway.org/index.php?pr=RTL_Infant_Brain_Devel (accessed March 17, 2007).

CHAPTER 10

1. Peters, Tom, and Nancy Austin, *A Passion for Excellence: The Leadership Difference* (New York: Warner Books, 1985).

2. Genesis 1:3 (ESV)

3. Acts 20:35 (ESV)

CHAPTER 16

1. Philippians 4:8 (ESV)

Sharing

MAKES CHILD CARE BETTER FOR EVERYONE.

Jean McCracken wrote *Peace with Child Care* to help parents find the best child care available - and then help it become even better. If you found this book helpful, please consider sharing this discount code with a friend to help her child benefit, too. *See reverse for details...*

20% Off

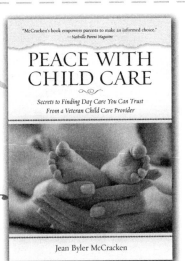

Sharing

MAKES CHILD CARE BETTER FOR EVERYONE.

Jean McCracken wrote *Peace with Child Care* to help parents find the best child care available - and then help it become even better. If you found this book helpful, please consider sharing this discount code with a friend to help her child benefit, too. *See reverse for details...*

20% Off

Get 20% Off the *Peace with Child Care* cover price with this online discount code when you purchase from Jean's website, www.PeaceWithChildCare.com.

20% Off

`share20241` *Enter this Online Discount Code at Checkout.*

This discount code is valid for an online purchase only and only at www.PeaceWithChildCare.com. Void where prohibited. Limit one per customer. Not for use in conjunction with any other offer. Not valid for prior purchases and not negotiable or redeemable for cash. Valid through **5/01/2008**.

Get 20% Off the *Peace with Child Care* cover price with this online discount code when you purchase from Jean's website, www.PeaceWithChildCare.com.

20% Off

`share20240` *Enter this Online Discount Code at Checkout.*

This discount code is valid for an online purchase only and only at www.PeaceWithChildCare.com. Void where prohibited. Limit one per customer. Not for use in conjunction with any other offer. Not valid for prior purchases and not negotiable or redeemable for cash. Valid through **5/01/2008**.